THE LAST HONEST PLACE IN AMERICA

THE LAST

Paradise and Perdition

HNEST

in the New Las Vegas

PLACE IN

MARC COOPER

AMERICA

Nation Books
New York

THE LAST HONEST PLACE IN AMERICA:
Paradise and Perdition in the New Las Vegas

Copyright © 2004 by Marc Cooper
Photographs copyright © 2004 by Anne Fishbein

Published by
Nation Books
An Imprint of Avalon Publishing Group
245 West 17th Street, 11th Floor
New York, New York 10011

Nation Books is a co-publishing venture of the Nation Institute and
Avalon Publishing Group Incorporated.

Library of Congress Cataloging-in-Publication Data is available.

ISBN 1-56025-490-4

9 8 7 6 5 4 3 2 1

Design by Simon M. Sullivan

Printed in the United States of America
Distributed by Publishers Group West

*To the memory of Neil Postman—for his ability to see
through the glare and hear beyond the clatter.*

CONTENTS

Introduction:
Las Vegas, America

A S A YOUNG BOY in the '50s and throughout my adolescence into the '60s, I would always feel that giddy anticipation starting to build as soon as my parents' car would finish gassing up in the dusty, California desert town of Baker, two-thirds of the way between Los Angeles and Las Vegas.

From the parking lot of the Bun Boy restaurant, famous for its strawberry waffles, there was still in front us a grueling forty-minute ride uphill toward Clark Mountain and the Nevada border, often with summer temperatures above 110 and with the attendant concerns of radiator boil-over.

Then, at the summit of 4,700 feet, the road finally flattening out, we'd glide through the flyspeck settlement of Mountain Pass distinguished only by a jumble of earth-colored machinery, and next, still in California, and making a sharp descending curve right at the turnoff for Nipton, we'd be confronted with an awesome, sweeping view of the oceanic desert to our east. The panorama unfolded as a wall of purplish-brown mountains with rose-ochre skirts to our right, rippling mahogany hills to our left, and straight in front of us, the sandy desert flats of pastel beige, tangerine, and pink stretching through Ivanpah Valley and then ever deeper into Nevada. The black stripe of Interstate 15 ripped right through its heart and on the hottest of summer days the smell of the bubbling, sticky asphalt would pour right into the cab of our red Plymouth Valiant.

This was the fabled "Baker Stretch"—the last, lonely, fifty-mile leg into Las Vegas. The view was essentially unpopulated desert as Vegas itself lurked behind another set of mountains. There was no suggestion of its presence except, of course, at night when its unrivaled batteries of lights along the casino Strip faintly silhouetted the dark mountains with an otherworldly, atomic-like glow.

But from the summit of the Stretch, no more than ten miles away on the looming horizon, was one small clump of civilization—of a sort. The minuscule hamlet of State Line was little more than a two-pump gas station, a wooden windmill, a ramshackle dozen motel rooms, one reddish neon sign, and a mom-and-pop convenience store all plunked down in the middle of nowhere, still forty miles shy of pulsating Las Vegas Boulevard but just a few feet across the Nevada border.

Unremarkable was State Line, by every measure. It was nearly indistinguishable from the other nearby pinpoint towns of Nipton and Searchlight, but with one all-important difference. The store at State Line had a single (or was it double?) row of noisy, boxy, vintage, green, gray, and dull-scarlet triple-reel stepper slot machines. This clapboard store was the first casino that travelers from California would encounter on the way to Vegas.

The origins of State Line reside in legend. One version has it that it came to being as State Line Station, a lone water tank along the tracks of Montana Senator William Clark's San Pedro, Los Angeles & Salt Lake Railroad (one of the major engines of southern Nevada's development). What is certain in that sometime in the 1920s, a grouchy miner named "Whiskey Pete" McIntyre set up shop, offering gas and bootleg booze to road-worn Angelenos making their Vegas pilgrimages. McIntyre died of miner's lung in 1933 and yet one more legend says he was buried standing up right along the interstate roadside.

Around the time I first came to State Line in the early 1950s, gambler Ernie Primm took over Whiskey Pete's gas station and store-casino. The operator of poker card-clubs in the gritty southern nether-region of Los Angeles County, Primm paid only $15,000 for the 400 acres of desert around State Line. Then for virtually no money, he acquired yet another 400 adjacent acres under the Federal Land-Grant Act. He snookered the Feds into the deal by technically complying with the act, passing himself off as a farmer, and actually planting fields of barley around the store that housed his slot machines.

In today's America, with gambling legal in nearly every state and Indian casinos as common as 7-Elevens, slot machines are themselves nowadays nearly as familiar as ATMs (though the money flow is reversed). But forty years ago, those one-armed bandits lined up neatly at State Line exercised a near totemic pull.

Our regular family treks to Las Vegas inevitably included ritualistic, almost baptismal-like stopovers in State Line. As if he were prepping for action in the Vegas casinos just ahead, my father would purchase a handful of rolls of silver dollars (talismans that seemed to circulate nowhere in America except in

Nevada casinos) and would start feeding them into the machines. And given the close confines of the State Line "casino," even as a minor, I could get damn close to the action. Close enough to decipher the spinning triple reels of oranges, pears, cherries, and plums. The *kerplunk* of the dollars into the machine, the *click-lock* of the handle coming down and snapping back, the ensuing *whir* and the infrequent clatter of more coins dropping into the metal retainers below were all unmistakable signals to me that—having arrived in State Line—we had not only crossed the border of California, but that we had at least temporarily departed from America. And from its daily strictures and norms. Standing at the slots, my father was no longer a mere steel salesman, my mother no longer just captain of her Tuesday-morning bowling team. For those moments, at least, they were of a much more exotic species. They were gamblers. And they were gambling in the only place on the continent where there was no risk of jail. And yet, all this vice seemed more than vaguely forbidden.

Win or lose in State Line, the rest of the ride into Las Vegas would be buoyant.

The classic attraction that Las Vegas has exercised on outsiders is precisely that it's always been a town where it's legal to be illegal. Even as a youngster I knew that the country's only licensed bordellos were a short drive from State Line in the town of Pahrump and that the glittering Vegas casinos were run by gun-toting gangsters and financed by crooked goon-ridden unions. Just hanging over the casino rail watching the slot machine reels spin, hearing cheers rise from the craps table or sitting by the pool at the Stardust, the Sands or the Hacienda, and recognizing the name of this or that legendary mobster or of Sid Caesar or Louis Prima being paged, was an exhilarating sort of a devilish sinfulness for an eleven-year-old from the L.A. suburbs. It sure beat the hell out of watching Sheriff John or Engineer Bill on black and white TV.

Now, more than forty years later, I'm back on what have become fairly regular sojourns in Vegas, standing on the the fifty-sixth floor of the open-air Ghost Bar, at the summit of the newest hotel and casino in town—the Palms. After serving as host to a recent series of MTV's *Real World* episodes, it's become this season's hottest ticket in Vegas. So hot that even on a slow Tuesday night in the dog days of summer, with nothing to offer but pricey drinks, ear-splitting techno, and startling views, it can still command a ten dollar cover charge just to get in the door.

As I stand on the bar balcony facing east toward the legendary Strip it's 2:30 A.M., but I'm surrounded by a pulsating swarm of mostly young people, many on their first visit here, bubbling and strutting and guzzling strawberry margaritas and iced tumblers of Jack or Jim. Some puff inexpertly on cigars while others loudly trade tales of drinking till dawn, of partying hearty over at the Hard Rock casino, of getting lap-danced over at Crazy Horse Too, or of blowing through stacks of five-dollar "nickel" chips at the cold-green Blackjack tables, or of pumping roll after roll of silver dollars into the insatiable video poker machines that jam the casino floor below.

I pay little attention to the boastful chatter as the explosion of lights below and in front and all around hold me mesmerized. The balmy desert night seems nuclear-lit. And though I have come here scores of times since those days when my parents would pack me along and I have seen Vegas grow and grow again and some more, I am nevertheless agog at the electric dazzle and buzz from this towering vantage.

Pitch black above, but to all four corners of the horizon, a raging blaze of light. From a city of maybe seventy-five thousand pitched into a tizzy during those three months in 1960 when the Rat Pack moved in to film the original *Ocean's Eleven*, the town has metastasized into a million-and-a-half, growing faster than any place on the continent, and doubling in population every decade.

From within that glimmering sea of lights emerge the usual sprawl of strip malls, car lots, supermarkets and big box discount stores now yellowishly glowing in the night. But floating in the middle of the lights is the crown-jewel attraction: the four-mile-long "Strip" of mega-resorts along Las Vegas Boulevard flickers and shamelessly beckons. It's the Mecca that lures an annual 37 million visitors who crowd in by plane, bus and car to offer up their $12 billion in tribute. Indeed, not even the real Mecca draws as many annual visitors. Disney World no longer pulls in as many tourists. Apart from the dozen mega-hotels on the strip, there are another 125 or so casinos in town. The twenty biggest hotels in the world are here. And just on the one corner of Flamingo Road and Las Vegas Boulevard, there are now more hotel rooms than in all of San Francisco.

Two striking pillars of light stand sentinel on both extremes of the Strip. On its southern edge, from the top of the Luxor Hotel's glass pyramid, the world's most powerful artificial light burns a laser beam visible to spacecraft orbiting more than 250 miles above the earth. On the northern edge, the 1,149-foot Stratosphere, a space-needle like tower which is the tallest structure west of the Mississippi, and now crowned with a restaurant, a wedding chapel, and a roller coaster, and illuminated with god-knows-how-much candlepower, gleams like a giant ivory phallus.

Between those two points stretch the dozen mammoth-sized

heavily "themed" resort-hotel boxes, each one a neon-lit display of what some call "architainmet." From this view point, the color coding of each property stands out against the night sky.

And as if they comprised some sort of giant glow-in-the-dark beaded rosary, I can mentally click through each casino and evoke one or another moment that has been burned into my memory. None of these experiences can be called transcendental, nor even vaguely weighty. They are instead rather banal, yet indelible.

Gazing at the purplish glow of the mid-strip Stardust, I remember a night almost thirty years ago, back at the time when Frank "Lefty" Rosenthal—the inspiration for Sam "Ace" Rothstein, the DeNiro character in *Casino*—was managing the place. The psychotic Anthony "The Ant" Spilotro (played by Joe Pesci in the film) was the street enforcer for the Midwest outfit that effectively owned the Stardust. It was the first time I was old enough to sit at the tables. After a few too many White Russians, my mother—a Vegas devotee—shot off her mouth at the Blackjack table, asking the pit boss for a five-thousand-dollar credit marker that she was sure she wouldn't get. To both of our amazement, he complied and shoveled us over a stack of black $100 chips. Within an hour we had lost most of it and I knew we had no way to pay it off. For ten more grueling hours, the two of us grinded away at the same table until we won it all back. We paid back the marker but didn't have enough to rent a room and wound up sleeping in my mother's white 1965 Cadillac.

The flickering torches at the Treasure Island remind me of a long interview inside with casino mogul Steve Wynn's then-PR flack in which he tried to convince me that commercial cynicism was a thing of the past in the "new Las Vegas" and that Sin City was poised to be a new "family destination resort."

The golden glow of the Mirage next door is indelibly associated with the worst losing streak I ever experienced. Sitting with my former agent David Vigliano in 1993 at a low-stakes Blackjack table, but one equipped with one of Wynn's new and diabolical automatic shuffling machines, I blew two thousand dollars in forty-five minutes—and this at a ten-dollar table.

At the pinkish Flamingo I recall an entire day spent trying to figure out the best strategy for playing Caribbean Stud Poker, a diabolical invention that allows the casino to win not only when the dealer has a good hand, but also a bad one. I did so peering at the cards with only one eye, my other eye covered with a pirate's patch clouded by a blood vessel burst by the stress of a three-day Vegas jag that prevented any sleep.

The newly built two-billion-dollar Venetian, with its white and brown detailing, warmly glimmers in the evening heat. On a recent visit I netted seventeen hundred dollars from its double-deck Blackjack tables.

But this is of course one of the few exceptions. "Give me a player for six days and I guarantee he'll leave a loser," says a Mandalay Bay pit executive. Stay long enough and you are bound to lose, and the edge the house maintains in every game offered will inevitably prevail. Come back here often enough and you can prove it easily enough to yourself.

So why do I keep returning? Why continue to trek back to a city whose motive for existence is to better separate me from my money? It can't be just the gambling. I've never made a bet outside of a casino. I don't take big risks with money. Nor am I terribly interested in the hundreds of casinos that have mushroomed in dozens of other states over the last decade. No. The allure of and the fascination with Las Vegas operates at a much deeper, almost visceral level

This book attempts to understand what pull this city exercises over me, if not over the tens of other millions who increasingly stream into its casinos, clubs, and resorts. And if not to fully understand that appeal, my goal, at least, is to measure its dimensions.

I found the period following the terrorist attacks of Sepember 11, 2001 to be an opportune historic moment to undertake this task. Las Vegas, after all, was now supposed to be everything we Americans were putting aside in this new chapter of history thrust so suddenly and rudely upon us. We were, after the collapse of the World Trade Center towers, said the media, less frivolous, more serious, less ironic, more authentic. How would Las Vegas, with all is bombast and artifice, fit into this post-9/11 America?

To answer that question, I made a few short trips to Las Vegas from my southern California home shortly after 9/11. And then from late 2002 into the summer of 2003, I spent longer and more frequent stretches of time in Vegas, sometimes weeks at a time, moving from one hotel to another, from the glitzy Strip to the frayed downown. As I got deeper into the research, it became ever more difficult to separate this work from the rest of my life.

Vegas is purposefully constructed as a self-enclosed and isolated biosphere, sort of what a recreational colony built on the moon might be like. This sense of timelessness and placenessless, if you will, often consumed me, rendering it quite arduous to distinguish if I was beginning or ending this project, if I was, in fact, working or just playing Blackjack, researching or just staying up all night because I was afraid to sleep.

One thing for sure, the reporting of this book was always accompanied by the low-level fever that Vegas induces, that resonant, electrified hum that—after sufficient exposure—inevitably replaces your normal body rhythms. Those times I got lost in Las Vegas, are probably the same moments when I stumbled closest upon its greater significance.

Vegas is often described as a city of dreams and fantasy, of tinselish make-believe. But this is getting it backward. Vegas is instead the American market ethic stripped completely bare, a mini-world totally free of the pretenses and protocols of modern consumer capitalism. As one local gambling researcher, Bo Bernhard, says gleefully: "What other city in America puts up giant roadside billboards promoting 97 percent guaranteed payback on slot play? In other words, you give us a buck and we'll give you back 97 cents. That's why I love my home town."

Even that stomach-churning instant when the last chip is swept away can be charged with an existential frisson. Maybe that's why they say that the difference between praying here and praying anywhere else is that here you really mean it. All the previous hours of over-the-table chitchat, of know-it-all exchanges between the ice-cool dealer and the cynical writer from the big city, the kibitzing with the T-shirted rubes and the open-shirted sharpies to my right and left, the false promises of the coins clanging into the trays behind me, the little stories I tell myself while my stack of chips shrinks and swells and then shrivels some more—all of this comes to an abrupt, crashing halt when the last chip goes back in the dealer's tray. No seats for the onlookers, sir.

And the other players at the table, the dealer who a moment ago was my buddy, the solicitous pit boss, the guy from Iowa in khaki shorts and topsiders peering over my shoulder, no longer give a fuck whether I live or die. And while winning is always better, even in moments of loss I feel a certain perverse thrill. It's one of the only totally honest interludes you have in modern America. All the pretense, all the sentimentality, the euphemisms, the hypocrisies, the come-ons, loss leaders, warranties and guarantees, all the fairy tales are out the window. You're out of money? OK, good—now get lost.

But in a city where the only currency is currency, there is a table-level democracy of luck in this realm of pay-as-you-play existence. Las Vegas is perhaps the most color-blind, class-free place in America. As long as your cash or credit line holds out, no one gives a damn about your race, gender, national origin, sexual orientation, address, family lineage, voter registration or even your criminal arrest record. Money is the great leveler. Just as it is the great hammer. For as long as you have chips on the table, Vegas deftly casts you as the star in an around-the-clock extravaganza. For all of America's manifold unfulfilled promises of upward mobility, Vegas is the only place guaranteed to come through—even if it's for a fleeting weekend. You may never, in fact, surpass the Joneses, but with the two-night-three-day special at the Sahara, buffet and show included, free valet parking and maybe a comped breakfast at the coffee shop you can certainly live like them for seventy-two hours—while never having to as much as change out of your flip-flops, tank top, and NASCAR cap.

What extraordinary prescience social critic Neil Postman displayed when he wrote in his 1985 book *Amusing Ourselves to Death* that Las Vegas—where Wall Street corporations had replaced mafias and mobs—should now be considered the "symbolic capital" of America. "At different times in our history," Postman wrote, "different cities have been the focal point of a radiating American spirit." In the era of the Revolutionary War, Boston embodied the ideals of freedom that would ring out first at Concord, Postman argued. Likewise, in the mid-nineteenth century "New York became the symbol of a melting-pot America." In the early twentieth century, the brawn and inventiveness of American industry and culture were captured in the energy of Chicago. "If there is a statute of a hog butcher somewhere in Chicago," Postman mused, "then it stands as a reminder of the time when America was railroads, cattle, steel mills and entrepreneurial adventures . . ."

"Today," Postman concluded, "we must look to the city of Las Vegas, Nevada as a metaphor of our national character and aspiration, its symbol a thirty-foot high cardboard picture of a slot machine and a chorus girl. For Las Vegas is a city entirely devoted to the idea of entertainment, and as such proclaims the spirit of a culture in which all public discourse increasingly takes the form of entertainment. Our politics, our religion, news, athletics, education and commerce have been transformed into congenial adjuncts of show business, largely without protest or even much popular notice."

When Postman penned these words nearly twenty years ago, little could he imagine that the Vegas he was writing about was the "old" Las Vegas and that Sin City was just a few years away from a radical makeover. Nor could Postman fully fathom that America itself was in the throes of a cataclysmic transformation. The more both places changed, the more they mirrored each other. Postman's hunch played out. And in spades.

Five years after Postman's book appeared, in 1989, Steve Wynn—with junk-bond financing from Michael Milken—stunned the Strip with his seven-hundred-million-dollar Mirage Hotel and Casino and touched off a revolution that brought about a scale and scope of spectacle hitherto unknown in human history. One after another, the old Rat Pack-era hotels would be dynamited and in their place would rise staggering leviathans of modern market-based entertainment: the biggest casino in the world, then the biggest hotel in the world, then the most expensive hotel in the world, the biggest man-made hotel lake in the world, the hotel with the biggest rooms in the world, and so on and so on.

If economist Joseph Schumpeter was correct in theorizing that "creative destruction is the essential fact about capitalism," then capitalism as practiced in Las Vegas is of the purest strain. The erection of the mammoth Vegas mega-resorts over the last dozen years was heralded not only by the televised dynamiting of their predecessors, but also accompanied by the concurrent collapse of much of the rest of America's urban and industrial and employment infrastructure. Isn't it logical or at least fitting that Las Vegas, the City of the Eternal Now, the town that seems to slather yet one more layer of pavement and glitz every few years over its own scant history, tradition, and roots would rise, just as long-entrenched communities from southeast Los Angeles to Lima, Ohio evaporated into the deindustrialized dust of globalization?

Indeed, just as quickly as Las Vegas consumes and erases the past and scrambles the present, it now shines to many as an attractive beacon of the future. Unlike almost any other place in America, Las Vegas today is one city where unskilled labor can still—thanks to vibrant unions and very wealthy and efficient employers—earn middle-class wages. Vegas food servers, car parkers, cashiers, even maids, can still buy right into the new American dream, purchasing a house and putting their kids through school. A high-school grad can become a professional dealer for three hundred bucks worth of tuition and a few weeks of practice pitching cards—and most likely get a job. Where else in America can you regularly find sixty-year-old bouffant-coifed cocktail waitresses proudly wearing union buttons (those of the mighty Culinary Workers Local 226) and going home to peruse the statements of their fattening pension accounts?

Some observers have gone so far as to call today's Vegas "the New Detroit." That's most probably an overstatement, as Las Vegas, unlike Motor City, produces nothing tangible. Instead, it discharges regular round-the-clock and alternating industrial-sized doses of hope and despair. Yet, the balance still tips decidedly in favor of the former. In an increasingly globalized economy, the human castoffs of de-industrialization find their last hope in the epicenter of the non-industrial economy, an economy at once infinitely more concrete and supremely more intangible than that of the dotcoms—Las Vegas.

In an American culture so disdainful of history, so obsessed with immediate emotional and sensual gratification, and in an economy that celebrates speculation over production, Las Vegas looks better than normal. It looks good. "Las Vegas as America, America as Las Vegas. It's like what came first? The chicken or the egg?" says Vegas historian Michael Green. "Fresno, California doesn't have a row of casinos but you can make sure it has some part of town where you can go for vice even though it's supposed to be illegal. Here it's not necessarily vice in the first place, but it's certainly not illegal. We have the same sort of stuff and more. Except that unlike in most places, here it's just out in the open."

At times over the last fifteen years it was as if a great, invisible hand had gripped the North American continent and tilted it upward to stand on the corner of southern Nevada, sending everyone and anyone else not solidly anchored to a middle-class job tumbling headlong toward Vegas. Even after the terrorist attacks on the World Trade Center slowed (slightly) what has traditionally been the recession-proof Vegas economy, a steady stream of five or six thousand domestic economic refugees a month still pour into the city. Only 6 percent of adults living in Vegas' Clark County were born here—the lowest such figure anywhere in America. And while water supplies are drying up, as the schools strain and as suicide and domestic-violence rates run among the highest in the nation, they keep pouring in. Purchasers for new homes—at prices far below the two coasts—are wait-listed. Over the decade of the '80s, its population doubled. And then doubled again in the '90s. Vegas continues to be fastest-growing metropolitan area in America.

This generation of immigrants, however, was different in many ways from the grifters, hustlers, and outcasts who had huddled here over the past century. Sure, there would always be a certain batch of trimmers, fugitives, and shake-down artists looking to launder themselves in the Vegas sun. But most of those who were now crowding into Las Vegas were fleeing from an America where everyday life had become too much of a gamble. Where either the Reagan recession of '81, the Bush slump of 1990, or the bubble-burst of a decade later had left them as devastated as a Blackjack player who had bet it all only to have his pair of tens get trounced by the dealer's ace-king. The only risk they were interested in now was the off-chance that Vegas—of all places—could provide the normalcy, the security, the certainty, that once anchored their lives, or at least their dreams.

What a turnaround it has been for once lowly Las Vegas—and for the nation around it. Barely fifteen years ago, the august Citicorp was queasy about publicly admitting that its major credit-card processing center had been relocated to an unincorporated suburb of Las Vegas. A deal with state authorities allowed the banking corporation to postmark and camouflage its mail as coming from "The Lakes, Nevada" instead of from sinful Vegas. Today, that same neighborhood sports several high-end casinos and luxury hotels. And Citicorp's own credibility, in the aftermath of the great Wall Street accounting scandals, ranks somewhere below that of a midtown three-card monte hustler.

Nor could Neil Postman know back in 1985 that casino gambling was about to be fully destigmatized within a decade—and delicately renamed "gaming." The resulting shift in public attitudes would not only definitively cleanse Vegas's image, but also net it an ongoing bonanza. As recently as 1988 casino gambling, or gaming, as it's called in the MBA programs, was legal only in Nevada and in Atlantic City, New Jersey. But as American industry continued to wash up offshore and the commercial tax base atrophied, one strapped state and municipality after another turned its forlorn eyes toward the gaming tables and slot machines. Impoverished Indian tribes were more than willing to sign gambling compacts with state governments. The result: now twenty-seven states have Nevada-style casinos. And forty-eight states have at least some form of legal gambling.

With local budgets again being squeezed by burgeoning deficits, government itself is now thinking about going into the casino business. In the spring of 2003, Chicago Mayor Richard Daley said he'd like to open a municipal casino. By the mid-1990s Americans were spending more on gambling than they were on movies. Before the 1989 opening of the Mirage unleashed the New Vegas revolution, only 15 percent of Americans had ever visited Las Vegas. By mid-decade that number had doubled. In its 1996 annual report Circus Circus celebrated the news: "In an era when social attitudes toward play, and the means to afford it, have dramatically changed, so has the role of the casino."

The last seven years has showed an ever more dramatic shift toward the mainstreaming of gambling. A gambling industry poll claimed that in the single year of 2001, fifty-one million Americans—more than a quarter of the population over age twenty-one—had visited a casino, chalking up a national total of almost three hundred million visits. More than 430 commercial casinos nationwide brought in $26.5 billon in revenue, two-and-a-half times what Americans spent on movie tickets, $5 billion more than on all DVDs and videos, and $3 billion more than they spent on all cosmetics and toiletries.

The explosion of legalized gambling nationwide has had little but positive impact on Las Vegas. "All it did was increase the average Joe's appetite for gambling," says a veteran Vegas Strip pit boss. "You know, it's like baseball. We see all those local Indian casinos and riverboat casinos and local slot parlors as our farm teams," he says. "They suck in a lot of average American types who never thought about gambling before. But once you play on the farm team, who doesn't want to play in the majors? And Las Vegas is the friggin' World Series. It's kind of like: you build the casinos out there and they'll come. But eventually they'll come here."

The difference between the marketing of Vegas a half-century ago and its marketing today is precisely the difference in mainstream American attitudes. "Fifty years ago, Lucille Ball was pregnant, and they couldn't say that word on *I Love Lucy*," says Green. "Today we have lesbian kisses on TV. We have the word 'bullshit' on prime time not to talk about cable programming. As the culture has become more open, Las Vegas can market itself more honestly." And, Green might add, there's a whole new line of Lucy-themed slot machines now out on casino floors.

In a time when Martha Stewart gets busted, Mark McGuire is on chemicals, and Sammy Sosa gets caught with a corker, against the cascade of recent corporate scandals, as everyday economic life in America has become a breathtaking risk, when it's an all-out crapshoot whether you still have a job next month, or whether your HMO will cover your spinal tap, or if you can hock the house for enough to pay for your kid's college tuition, and it's anybody's guess whether your company will renege on your private pension plan, well then, who can say whether it would have really been that stupid to have let it all ride on 18 Red? Was it smarter to invest ten years of savings in an Enron-backed 401(k) or to have better spent your time studying the probability charts for single-deck Black-jack? Is the integrity of the roulette wheels at the Bellagio more tainted than the quarterly corporate reports coming out of WorldCom? Both are iffy propositions. But at least in Vegas the rules of the game are clear-cut and transparent, the industry is tightly regulated, and the unfavorable odds are clearly and publicly posted. There are no multi-million-dollar-a-year cable TV touts telling you that red or black or double-zero green is the next, best thing or that Life somehow owes you an eternal double-digit annual return from your dabblings in dice.

Haven't we, in fact, reached a point in our culture where the button-down bankers and arbitrageurs have become the reckless "casino capitalists" while those who actually run the casinos can get away labeling themselves responsible and conservative "entertainment visionaries"—even if they are, increasingly, often the same people?

A couple of years back at a gambling industry convention in Las Vegas, the Chief Financial Officers of three major casinos sat on a public panel. When someone from the floor asked if investment in the casino business was a good bet, one of the CFOs answered, essentially: the difference between us and Enron is that at least our money is real.

That globally recognized icon of Las Vegas, the neon-lit, hand-waving cowboy, Vegas Vic, unveiled in 1947 and still presiding over downtown's Fremont Street, used to regularly and electronically call out "Howdy, pardner" until the complaints of card-groggy hotel guests had him permanently muted. But if Vic could speak today, he might as well be saying, "Welcome to Las Vegas, pardner. The last honest place in America."

THE LAST
HONEST
PLACE IN
AMERICA

Part One

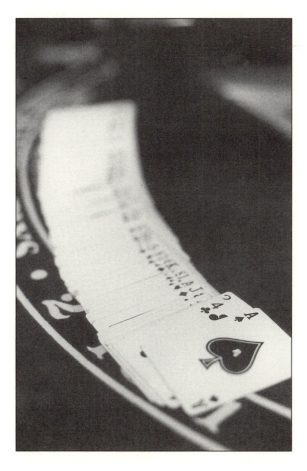

Vegas Is Dead. Viva Las Vegas!

IT'S 1:45 A.M. ON the warm morning of October 23, 2001, barely six weeks after the World Trade Center disaster, and there's little public appetite to applaud the violent downing of another tall building. But here along the perpetually bright Vegas Strip, a crowd of hundreds, about a half-dozen deep, have nevertheless assembled, and they quietly, almost somberly, wait for the top of the hour. At precisely 2 A.M., the newspapers say, a switch will be thrown, 248 pounds of explosives will be triggered, and the bare-metal-and-concrete skeleton of the once mighty 15-story Augusta Tower of the Desert Inn—the fifth luxury resort ever built in Las Vegas, and what some consider to have been the city's ultimate embodiment of cool—will be reduced to dust.

Compared to the hoopla and media frenzy that surrounded the blowing up of other Vegas hotels over the past decade, the demolition of the Desert Inn seems, at first blush, little more than a historical asterisk. Vegas readily cashed in on previous implosions. When the Hacienda went down on New Year's Eve 1996 a street party was thrown and dubbed "Dynamite New Year" and televised live on Fox while tens of thousands watched from the sidewalks. The demolition of Howard Hughes's failed Landmark Hotel was filmed by Hollywood for use in *Mars Attacks!* The crumbling Sands Hotel made it onto the cover of *Harper's* magazine. And when the old Aladdin was killed off in 1998 its owners charged spectators $250 a head for a close-up view of the demolition from a V.I.P. tent.

The dynamiting of the D.I., however, is to be carried out in the dark of night with virtually no fanfare. And it's not just squeamishness over the recent 9/11 attacks that's led to such furtiveness. There's almost a sense of guilt, maybe shame—if either of those two emotions are still allowed here.

Under any circumstances, this patch of soulless desert seems about the last place on Earth to get weepy about. Lamenting the disappearance of any part of history in this city that consistently shakes off historic timelines like a bad coat of fleas is bound to be met with nothing more than raised eyebrows and shrugs.

But I confess that my stomach knots as I see how the once exquisite Desert Inn has been disfigured and disemboweled in preparation for her beheading. Caged by a chain-link storm fence, her entire southern flank has been bashed in, her skin peeled off, her insides gutted and flayed, now splayed open to the indifferent passersby. Toothy orange forklifts and bulldozers surrounding her like metallic piranha have chewed out her bottom floors, exposing the spindly I-beams that barely still hold her erect. The tangle of pipes, ducts, tubes, and cables that I saw grotesquely dangling near the ground a few weeks ago have now been covered with a funereal black drape.

The ultimate indignity? Part of her cream-ivory-colored corpse has been splotched wth a garish coat of rouge, a remnant from earlier this year when the elegant lady was forced to appear as an extra in the abominable film *Rush Hour 2*.

Once the fuses are lit forty minutes from now, the D.I. will enter the unmarked graveyard of the other imploded Strip hotels. But those casinos met their end when each was tired, if not exhausted, worn down and overcome by time. The Desert Inn is different. It goes down just a few years after a glorious remodeling and makeover—and after she was seduced, betrothed, acquired, and then hastily betrayed by the most powerful and richest man in town. And her demise marks the end of a historic era in a city that denies there is any past, or any future beyond your arrival and departure dates—and the expiration of your line of credit.

"Go to a European hotel, and they brag about it being three hundred years old," says Dick Taylor, who managed the Hacienda when it first opened, a few years after the D.I. "But not here, man. No one cares that Sinatra lived in Room 124 of the Sands. They don't care about the Sands. They don't care about the Desert Inn. Here, when you hit age fifty, they just blow you up."

The Desert Inn and I came into the world together in the same year, 1950. When my parents would bring me here, we'd stay at El Rancho Vegas, the Hacienda, the Stardust and later the Dunes. Not until I was an adult did I encounter the D.I. And when I did, I fell hard and hopelessly for her. Since then, I would seek any excuse for making the four-hour drive to spend an impromptu weekend, a night, even a long single afternoon in her fragile embrace.

The D.I.'s allure was formidable. All around her, the latest

Disneyfied gimmicks planted on the Strip noisily jostled for attention: the white tigers and volcano of the Mirage, the live action pirate ship "battle royal" at the Treasure Island, the shark tank at the Mandalay, or the dancing fountains at the Bellagio. Even the once august Caesar's Palace felt compelled by the competition to build a shopping mall that awed the crowds with talking statues.

The D.I. had none of the above, fortunately. She was the last surviving refuge, the final holdout of understated elegance and Old Vegas class and cool left on the Strip. A few other Old Guard hotels and casinos still operated on the Strip—the Frontier, the Stardust, the Sahara, the Riviera. But they survive only by effectively serving as low-rent dormitories—featuring cheap room-rates and nickel slots—for underbudgeted tourists wanting to glimpse the glitzier new generation mega-resorts on the lower half of the Strip but not having the cash to stay in them. Who could have imagined back in the era of Frank and Sammy that the once-exotic Sahara would eventually adopt a NASCAR theme and sully its casino with one-dollar Blackjack tables?

Not the D.I. It bravely held its ground, living the apparent delusion that adults might still want a playground of their own, one they didn't have to share with their kids. Perhaps one pristine little piece of this America where you were *not* expected to eat with your hands and *not* expected to wear your tennis shoes. With no special effects, no shtick—no bullshit—the Desert Inn immersed you in the most intoxicating of all Vegas fantasies: Las Vegas itself, Sin City. That's at least how the D.I. hooked me. I'm not adverse to admitting a certain indulgence in fantasies. But if I'm going to travel three hundred miles across a desert to a town designed primarily to suck me dry of money, I want to get something out of the exchange. I don't want to pretend I'm a pirate, or a Roman slave, or a medieval knight, an Arabian sheik, an island castaway, a shark tamer, or a race-car driver. If I wish to visit the Piazza San Marco, or the Eiffel Tower, or glimpse the Manhattan skyline, I prefer the real thing over the scale model. And I certainly don't want to hand my money over to a fresh-out-of-correspondence-school dealer wearing a balloon sculpture on his head or dressed in a gold-lamé toga. I'll leave all that for when the visiting cousins want a day in Disneyland. Or for just about any other modern "entertainment experience" in America.

I go to Las Vegas—or at least I went to Las Vegas—because even though I knew everything that was sinister, calculating, and evil about it, I loved Las Vegas. Only in Vegas could I dare to fantasize that I was a Friend of Frank. Or that I was throwing the dice at Dino's favorite table. Or that I might luck out and sip bourbon with Rickles after his last lounge show. The D.I. oozed that kind of heady fantasy. The kind of Rat Pack Cool that Hollywood defiled and butchered when it remade *Ocean's Eleven* a few years ago. (Substituting George Clooney for Frank Sinatra, lots of close-ups of icy cold techno-gadgets and an overload of cyber-jabber for the schmoozing and boozy banter among the original cast. Come back Peter Lawford, all is forgiven).

Once inside the doors of the D.I., I knew I was safely delivered from the swelling, heat-stricken herds of shorts-clad schleppers outside grazing the Strip, fanny-packs around their waists, one hand clasped around a twenty-four-ounce watermelon margarita souvenir glass, one eye fixed on the video-cam viewfinder, the other on the pulsating Circus Circus sign that reeled them in with ninety-nine-cent shrimp cocktails.

The mere scarcity of slot machines at the D.I. was the greatest deterrent to the fanny-packers. The Desert Inn, thankfully, ranked twenty-second among the twenty-two major Strip casinos in slot count—barely four hundred machines, and even those were mercifully gagged and muted—no bells, sirens, or synthesized tones burping all around you. (By comparison, some casinos have six or seven that number of slots). The result was the two most rarefied of modern Vegas commodities—lots of quiet, and lots of actual gambling tables—which meant that if you were going to gamble, then at least you had to sit down with other players, talk to a human dealer, pull out enough money to crank up your heart rate into the target zone, and get ready to remember at least the basic few rules of craps or Blackjack. If you preferred instead to plop down, zone out, and blithely pump nickels into a video machine that paid off when you lined up the proper configuration of animated bunny rabbits, squirrels, squashes, and carrots, then you just kept on moving toward the Riv, or you took a left toward the Palace Station, but you didn't set foot inside the D.I.

At the D.I., I wouldn't dare come to the table without a suit and tie. Anything less formal might offend the seasoned dealers who stood behind their tables in starched white shirts and perfectly knotted black bow ties. Mostly middle-aged men and women, usually with twenty years of dealing behind them, a recognized elite in a city full of freshly minted dealers and croupiers, their wrists and pinkies flashing with gold and ice, they would call you by your name and listen to you with at the least the feigned interest of a therapist. When the occasional rube walked in and threw away a stack of twenty-five-dollar green "quarter" chips by splitting tens and hitting dead hands when the house was showing a five or six up, the dealer would inevitably share a knowing glance with the more experienced players. And there I would sit at one of the Blackjack tables, hours at a time, savoring the quiet shuffle of the cards, soothed by the low lighting, the high, domed ceiling, the gentle indoor palms, the hushed and polished Monte Carlo décor, drifting toward dawn, often straight into the morning, sometimes winning, more often not. But who cared? The treatment was so tender that even at the frayed end of a losing streak, I almost had the urge to stand up, straighten my tie, and shake the dealer's hand, thanking him—or her—for spending this time with me.

All that was now about to be blown into rubble at the corner of Las Vegas Boulevard and Desert Inn Road, where nostalgia, memory, and tradition intersect and finally collide with the corporate bottom line.

From its very conception inside Wilbur Clark's head, the Desert Inn was to outclass the rest of the Strip.

Clark, whose early gambling career took him from San Diego to Manhattan Beach and, most probably, to the infamous Rex gambling boat that once sat anchored off the shores of Santa Monica, was by the mid-1940s already dabbling with investments in then-budding Las Vegas. According to historian Jack Sheehan, "Wilbur Clark had dreamed up an idea for a palatial casino resort, the Desert Inn—a name he borrowed from a motel in Palm Springs." The southern California desert oasis was a major link in the naional archipelago of clandestine gambling centers.

In 1947, when Las Vegas had maybe 4000 residents, Clark started rustling up funding for his dream project, but he was never able to put together more than a quarter million, a small fraction of what he would need. He found himself in the same fix that haunted another Californian at roughly the same time. Billy Wilkerson, publisher of the *Hollywood Reporter,* had also hatched the idea of a luxury resort on the lonely strip of highway outside downtown Las Vegas that led back to L.A. When Wilk-erson ran out of money he turned to Benjamin "Bugsy" Siegel who, with godfather Meyer Lansky's millions, conjured up the Flamingo which opened in the Christmas of 1946.

"The D.I. is a whole story like the Flamingo," Frank Wright, the former curator of the Nevada State Museum told me shortly before his death in 2003. "The D.I.'s inspiration came from a Californian who eventually had to turn to the mob." The under-world sugar daddy Clark turned to was yet another Lansky asso-ciate, Morris Barney "Moe" Dalitz, leader of Cleveland's Jewish mob. He, in turn, tapped his pal Jimmy Hoffa and with backing from the Teamsters Central States Pension Fund, Dalitz and his outfit snapped up 74 percent of the D.I. and laid out $3.4 million to finish it.

From the moment the resort opened in the Spring of 1950, both the Desert Inn—known officially as Wilbur Clark's Desert Inn—and its real operator, Moe Dalitz, were heading for history. (Within a year of the resort's opening Clark's role, meanwhile, was "reduced to checking that his name was still on the match-books and napkins," says historian Hal Rothman).

The D.I. immediately became synonymous with elegance. "From its first days, the D.I. maintained a constant identity as a venue with class," said Wright. *Life* magazine reported that its opening gala was attended by "almost everybody who amounts to anything in Nevada." Its 225 rooms were the first to have indi-vidually controlled thermostats. The swimming pool was a figure eight. A fountain shot water more than fifty feet in the air. In pre-moonshot America, this was the pinnacle of spectacle.

The rooftop, glass-enclosed Sky Room bar and lounge was the A-list hangout, quite literally, as it would draw raucous, boozy, standing-room crowds who'd come to cheer and toast the flash and rumble of at least some of the first of the 126 open-air atomic tests detonated between 1951 and 1962 at the nearby Nevada Testing Site. Soon, it's said, the A-bomb tests became so frequent in Southern Nevada that they were routinely ignored. But at first the Desert Inn's Sky Room hosted what were called "dawn parties"— drinking and singing marathons that would begin after midnight and culminate at sun break with an atomic blast. Back in 1952 a D.I. waitress described the scene at the Sky Room bar: "It was a wonderful place for what the customers wanted. They could sit around and listen to our piano player and look out the big windows and see the pretty hotel fountain and the guests swimming in the pool and the traffic speeding by on Highway 91, and then, just when they were starting to get tired, the A-bomb."

Dalitz might have been a ruthless mobster but he was also recognized as a brilliant hotelier and casino strategist. Long before anyone had heard of Steve Wynn, Dalitz figured out that giving the customer the highest-end treatment at an accessible price was the path to success. And he correctly guessed that visiting gamblers wanted more than casino action. The D.I. opened a world-class golf course and it was Dalitz who dreamed up the Tournament of Champions, a PR plus for Vegas. Wilbur Clark not only lent credibility to Dalitz, but was also an effective front man for the city itself. "He was seen as Mister Clean," said Wright. "Wilbur Clark gave me my first job in Las Vegas. That was in 1951," Frank Sinatra said a handful of years before he died. "For six bucks you got a filet mignon dinner and me."

Dalitz's formula paid off big-time. In it first year alone, the D.I. casino made a cool three million dollars, almost three-fourths of the original capital investment.

Kenny Franks, now a blackjack supervisor at the downtown Binion's Horseshoe, broke in as a twenty-two-year-old dealer at the Desert Inn in 1957 and remembers it then as "a place that had more glamour than any place that ever existed in Vegas." His older cousin Frank Soskin was part of the original Cleveland outfit that opened the D.I. with Dalitz and he managed the casino for more than two decades. "The D.I. was so hot a place because the people who ran it had all the best connections. The best entertainment. The best tables. The highest limits. And while Wilbur Clark had only a small piece of it, he was the front guy, the guy you took your picture with. And he was great at it."

As the '50s passed, a building boom transformed Vegas and provided stiff competition for the D.I. But it continued to prosper and profit into the next decade. As did Dalitz. His success not only parallels that of the D.I. but is also symbolic of the overall transformation and evolution of Las Vegas in the immediate post-war period. There's that memorable scene in Francis Ford Coppola's *The Godfather* in which the young crime boss Michael Corleone, dressed in a long black coat and oversized black hat, is walking down a bucolic New England path, his matching black limousine trailing slowly behind, trying to convince his estranged lover to marry him. He vows "that within five years, Kate, the Corleone family will be 100 percent legitimate." That might as well have been Dalitz mouthing the same lines in the late '50s.

If never fully legal, Dalitz certainly became legit. At least by Vegas standards. In 1958 he shaved off the just-opened Stardust Hotel from Jake "The Barber" Factor. He exercised staggering local clout by advising Jimmy Hoffa on who should and should not benefit from Teamster loans and funding. Twenty years after opening the D.I., Dalitz had become one of the most respected benefactors in the city—despite a constant trickle of press exposés on his mob connections. But it was Dalitz who founded the city's premier hospital, the Sunrise—again with union cash—and his huge camapign contributions were eagerly sought by Nevada's most powerful politicians.

"I can't say enough about Dalitz," says former Hacienda manager Dick Taylor, a devout Mormon who now runs a small religious press. "Dalitz was a great guy. If you needed to build the YMCA, a community pool, anything like that, you went to Moe. He would open his drawer and pull out a stack of hundreds. Dalitz did it because it's like Dalitz had a license to print money."

In 1976 Dalitz was named Humanitarian of the Year by the American Cancer Research Center. The Anti-Defamation League of the B'nai B'rith gave him its highest award in 1982. And when Dalitz died in 1989, more than a dozen nonprofit groups split $1.3 million he had put aside in a charitable trust.

But his greatest legacy, the one Vegas institution most closely associated with his name, remained the Desert Inn. In 1966, the eccentric billionaire Howard Hughes took up residence on the D.I.'s top floor. After several gentle suggestions from management that he move out, Hughes plunked down $13.5 million the next year and ostensibly took over the hotel—though Dalitz still ran it for a time. Hughes died a decade later and by then his Summa Corporation firmly controlled the property.

By the mid-1980s, the D.I. was still second or third in the Vegas market, and though no one could discern it at the time, its eventual fate was already being cast. Las Vegas had already massified its appeal by lowering the bars of formality in the casinos and offering $4.99 dinner buffets. By the time computer technology livened up the slot machines, showrooms began operating more as movie houses than nightclubs, and Vegas became a low-roller heaven.

To keep its high-end niche in the market, the D.I. began

recruiting players from overseas. But just as Summa sold Wilbur Clark's original property to entrepreneur Kirk Kerkorian in 1988, a marketing earthquake was coming that would rejigger Las Vegas, expunge its lingering past as Sin City, and eventually take down the D.I.

Vegas's Mirage Age commenced with a deafening boom—the dynamiting of the Dunes to make room for Steve Wynn's mega-resort, the most extravagant theme hotel the town had ever seen and a property that would influence everything Vegas has built since. The Mirage opened in 1989 and was immediately making more than $1 million a day in profits. Disneyism had come to the desert—and it worked, leveling everything that had come before it.

"The Mirage changed everything overnight," says Bill Sou, who worked at the D.I. in the 1980s recruiting big rollers, "whales" as they are known, from overseas and who is today a vice president at the Mirage. "As soon as Steve [Wynn] opened the Mirage, it sucked off all the big players. It hit us at the D.I. very hard. It rocked Caesar's Palace. It killed off everything high and low."

As a string of Disneyfied resorts opened—the Luxor, Treasure Island, the Excalibur, etc.—the staid, Rat Pack-era properties were brusquely pushed from the spotlight. The D.I. ownership shifted to Sheraton, but knowing virtually nothing of the casino business it eschewed the new populism. As the other hotels pandered to the lowest common denominator, the D.I. came up with a fifty-dollar Sunday buffet that offered three types of caviar.

And then what can only be called a miracle—at least by the rules of Vegas—occurred. In 1997 the hotel's owners put the property through a two-hundred-million-dollar remodelling. Initial rumors were that the D.I. was going to add thousands of rooms and become the biggest of the new breed of New Vegas resorts.

But somehow, against all odds, at the precise moment when Vegas was bathed in schlock, the remodeled D.I. reemerged gracefully updated, starkly elegant, and—in what must be the only case in Las Vegas history—smaller than before the remodelling. The hotel had shrunk from 821 rooms to 715. Downright cozy by Mirage Age yardsticks. The D.I.'s. new seven-story, marble-floored and palm-lined atrium lobby evoked the golden age of Palm Beach in the 1930s. Its casino remained uncluttered by slots and had the solid wood-and-brass feel of Monte Carlo. Its tables were still the quietest, most dignified, classiest swaths of green felt in town. The new Desert Inn was much like the old. It proffered no "attraction," no "adventure," no spectacle other than itself and its rich historic tradition.

But no good deed goes unpunished.

"The D.I. was trying to go for that top 2 percent elite. It said to itself, 'Let's do what we do best, what Moe Dalitz did best,'" says Dick Taylor. "But it just couldn't compete. It couldn't compete with the three- and four-thousand room behemoths right down the street." The D.I. had only luxury itself—and real Vegas gambling—to offer, and as a result was losing money. Everything that made the D.I. and its muffled, spacious, and dignified casino alluring to me was exactly what made it a guaranteed loser in the New Vegas.

Yet another shuffle of ownership transferred it to Starwood Hotels & Resorts Worldwide, whose management quickly put the lady on the auction block.

Then, in April 2000, for a bargain-basement price of $270 million, Steve Wynn himself snapped up the Desert Inn—as, he said, a birthday present for his wife.

The purchase allowed Wynn, who had just sold his Mirage Resorts (including the $2 billion Bellagio and the nearby Treasure

Island), to quickly get back into the hotel business. But it also cast an immediate chill on the Desert Inn's future. I sat at the Blackjack tables three weeks after the deal was announced, and the dealers spoke apprehensively of what was to come. Wynn had promised them at least a full year's moratorium before any decision about the hotel's fate would be made. But few believed it. They knew what was at stake, and they were rattled by his public statements. "This is the most powerful piece of real estate in Nevada, possibly in the western United States," Wynn said shortly after the deal was inked. "It's an extraordinary piece of property, with an opportunity to do just about anything."

The least likely thing he would do, his employees concluded, would be to keep the D.I. as it was. And they were right. On June 30, 2000 Wynn took formal ownership. Six weeks later he went back on his promise of a one year moratorium and gave the Desert Inn staff, many who had loyally worked there for decades, a mere fifteen days' notice. The casino would cease operations at 2 A.M. on Monday, August 28, 2000. The hotel would shut forever twelve hours later.

The last gambler to hold the dice at the "palatial resort" dreamed up by Wilbur Clark and birthed by Moe Dalitz was regular guest Fred Heitmann of Illinois, a man who commanded a thirty-thousand-dollar casino credit line at the casino. On what would turn out to be his final roll of the dice he had to make the number eight. But he struck out with an unlucky seven and contributed a final eight hundred dollars to the D.I.'s last "drop," the daily pile-up of cash.

A few courageous crusaders mounted a short-lived Internet site to save the D.I. from demolition. The campaign, predictably, went nowhere.

Shortly before the scheduled takedown of the D.I., Wynn

finally broke a long, self-imposed silence and spoke in some detail of his plans for the Desert Inn to one local Las Vegas reporter and again during a public speech at a casino trade expo. Wynn announced his plans to convert the old D.I. site into a new two-billion-dollar resort, Le Reve—in French, "The Dream"— named for the Picasso painting, which he, by the way, owns. With at least 2,500 rooms, a 514 foot tower, 42 stories, and a series of man-made lakes, the hotel would take approximately 30 months to build, he said. And in some faint recognition of the tradition of the Desert Inn, the new hotel will have no theme— other than elegance. "It's time for Las Vegas to have its own hotel," said the man responsible for demolishing the last great landmark hotel in town. Said Wynn of Le Reve: "People are going to come from everywhere to see it and marvel at it."

It's finally rolled around to 2 A.M. on this Tuesday morning in October, and as Steve Wynn himself—safe on the northern end of the D.I. property—prepares to push the appropriate detonation button, an anticipatory hush falls over the crowd. Suddenly it's the top of the hour. On the dot, the button is pressed and a staccato series of eight or nine booms sound out. A *rat-a-tat* of a dozen more pops resonate off the concrete canyon walls of the Strip. The iconic tower of the D.I. momentarily shimmies and shudders in a macabre death rattle and then, less than twenty seconds after the fuses ignite, she collapses and disappears under her own weight. From her gravesite rises a towering cloud of dust that, in the still, warm night air, drifts eastward ever so slowly toward and into the darkness of the surrounding desert.

"A lot of people say Las Vegas blows up its history. I'm not sure that's so true," says historian Michael Green. "Fact is, it's Steve

Wynn that's blown up more of Las Vegas than anyone else. It hurt me to see the Desert Inn and the Sands go because those two places were the epitome of Las Vegas in the '50s and '60s. But all this begs the question: Has Wynn blown up history? Or just blown up parts of the past we can easily replicate? You know, there's an old saying in this industry: 'A joint's a joint.' " Or, to put it more bluntly, as UNLV's Hal Rothman does, "Blowing up the Desert Inn doesn't mean shit to a tree."

Whatever its deeper meaning, if any, the demise of the Desert Inn as the last outpost of Vegas cool was preordained and inevitable—a predictable side-effect of the emergence of the New Las Vegas. There just wasn't any place anymore for the D.I. Burt Cohen, the D.I. casino's former president during three different stints, spoke to the *Las Vegas Sun* shortly after the implosion. And while he was clearly overstating both the past and the present, his lament nevertheless resonated deeply with the truths of changing times. "In the early days consumers never went to bed till three or four in the morning," he said. "They would see two shows, have a gourmet dinner, visit at least two lounge shows and in between be gambling, drinking booze, and chasing broads. As times passed, consumers changed—they would get up at seven in the morning and go jogging. Now, most of them are in bed by eleven or twelve o'clock."

Fear and Lava

T HE SCENE IS so Middle American wholesome that if Bugsy
Siegel or Moe Dalitz or any of the real city fathers were
to saunter by at the moment, I'm sure someone would
whip out his cell phone and call the cops. This is Ground Zero of
the New Vegas, halfway up the four-mile Strip staring straight
at the faux volcano rising fifty-four feet in front of the shimmering Mirage Hotel and Casino. If it's any day of the year
except maybe Christmas or Thanksgiving, and you trek here,
you'll be immersed in a colorful sea of fellow Americans sprin-
kled with a generous quota of foreigners. If it's sometime other
than the coldest day of winter, most will be wearing short pants.
Those fanny-packs, in basic black as well as hot pink and char-
treuse, so absent from the old Desert Inn, will now be so abundant that it will seem Vegas is host to a massive convention of
colostomy patients.

On a regularly scheduled cycle carefully calibrated to the flow of foot traffic, the volcano begins to belch and grumble as recorded sound effects issue forth from the weatherproof speakers hidden among the papier mâché boulders and rocks at its base. On cue, the fanny-packers, en masse, set their video camcorders to whirring and their digital cameras to clicking.

Frankly, you only know that this rumbling hi-tech structure in front of you is a volcano because that's what the management at the Mirage and all the guide books call it. To the untrained eye it comes off more as a squat, rather symmetrical, triple-tiered, earth-colored concrete pump-driven fountain-cum-waterfall that empties into an oversize dark-bottomed pool with a lot of pumice stone glued to its sides.

As the recorded soundtrack dramatically mounts, dozens of red floodlights flash on and off. A piped vent just clearing the top surface starts blowing out puffs of steam. A gas jet next to the steam pipe ignites and a large flame politely reaches toward the sky, simultaneously setting off five or six similar rows of gas burners running down the slope of the volcano slab and into the pool below, making the whole contraption appear as an oversized and badly damaged kitchen stove. The flames burn a gassy bluish-yellow for about a minute and then—suddenly—*poof!* The show is over. Though one cynical friend of mine said the whole thing reminded him of nothing more than his own childhood spent wandering among chemical cracking plants and industrial waste in Elizabeth, New Jersey, the culmination of each show inevitably draws loud applause and cheers from the assembled onlookers.

"It's an adult amusement park and that's why we come here," California visitor Cathy Keefer told a reporter recently after watching the volcano show. "We're not gamblers. We like the scenery."

Thousands of other like-minded tourists, day and night, make what you might call the Long March—walking, and when the mercury skims triple digits, dragging and trudging, up and down the Strip taking in, yes, this strictly man-made industrial strength "scenery." Next door to the Mirage, the landscape is dominated by Treasure Island's hourly pirate battle with booming, smoking cannons. Across the street, the costly replica of the Venice canals and Piazza San Marco at the Venetian, the one-half scale model of the Eiffel Tower at the Paris, the reproduction of the Manhattan skyline and its harbor at New York New York, the Giza Pyramids at the Luxor, the Moroccan desert at the mostly deserted and failing new Aladdin, the Italian lake district at the ultra-luxurious Bellagio, a taste (more like a drop) of Monaco at the middlebrow Monte Carlo, a South Seas getaway at the swank Mandalay Bay (which somehow features a posh post-Soviet Russian dinner house), or if all else fails, a celebration of rock and roll at the Hard Rock Hotel (with the image of Jimi Hendrix on its five dollar casino chips) or, the best of all stand-bys in American culture, the Hollywood-themed MGM Grand whose one-hundred-thousand-pound bronze lion statue takes a team of three people an entire week to clean and polish.

I'm not enough of a sociologist to fully comprehend what about all this creates such an irresistible gravitational pull on so many. Maybe, in a such an insular country as ours where less than 10 percent of the population has a passport, when so many Americans are hesitant to travel where English is not the lingua franca, it's as neat and simple as the way one Mirage executive summed it up. "They can travel the world in Las Vegas simply by walking the Strip," he said.

Undoubtedly the case. But the Strip also must tell us something about what cultural critics like Neal Gabler suggest is an entertainment overload; that more and more Americans find certain things "entertaining" because these experiences conform so obediently with now-ritualized formulas of entertainment that one feels almost compelled to validate them as such—even if they are not, in fact, very amusing. Something Gabler calls "like-entertainment." You laugh at a dull sitcom or *oooh* and *ahhh* at a mechanized volcano because you feel it is the expected thing to do. What, indeed, does a tourist, after returning home to Ohio or Pennsylvania, actually do with all that videotape he shot of the rubberized "rain forest" inside the Mirage lobby or of the talking statues inside Caesar's Forum? Do relatives and neighbors gathered in his living room actually enjoy watching a taped replay of the volcano explosion?

After I saw the Mirage volcano for the first time, I was brought back to the observations of Neil Postman. In a television-marinated society in which the boundaries between childhood and adulthood have been blurred if not erased, where, increasingly and dismayingly, children and adults dress the same, eat the same, and often talk the same, where they certainly endlessly watch the same TV shows, where simulation is often valued over authenticity (look no further than the acrobatic contrivances of so-called "reality TV" or the reclassification of steel and concrete hotels into "scenery"), it should come as little surprise that the phony lava eruption and the staged pirate-show next door should bring equal glee to ten-year olds *and* their parents. Add to that a certain solace Americans find in the worship of technology, even technology deployed at this infantile level, and the Strip begins to make perfect sense.

Predictably enough, those who have designed and operate the Strip have a much clearer-eyed view of this matter. The extravagant exteriors of the mega-resorts and the evolution of the Strip itself into one stretched-out spectacle "set a tone and also make a statement," said Alan Feldman, spokesman for MGM Mirage. "If the outside can be this fantastic, imagine what the inside must be like." In other words, we do all this to eventually get you inside the casino.

Once inside those casinos, or even gawking at them from the outside, how many tourists stop to ask themselves who the are owners? In a country where two-thirds of the population mistakenly thought Saddam Hussein had a direct role in 9/11, many of those who even take the time to pose the query probably conclude it's somehow still the Mafia or the underworld. They couldn't be more mistaken.

As in virtually every other facet of American business, the Las Vegas gambling industry is monopolized by a handful of companies who continue to merge, consolidate, and dwindle in number. A few are still controlled by powerful private families and individuals. Sheldon Adelson, for example, takes a hands-on approach to running his lavish Venetian Hotel and Casino. Other gambling giants are the most modern of Wall Street-traded corporations, including Ramada and Harrah's. And then there are the three corporations that constitute a veritable Strip oligopoly.

The MGM Mirage company—in part a hybrid of the former holdings of individual entrepreneurs Steve Wynn and current mogul Kirk Kerkorian—owns the Mirage, Treasure Island, Bellagio, MGM Grand, New York-New York, Golden Nugget, 50 percent of the Monte Carlo, and more than a half dozen other casinos in Vegas, other parts of Nevada, Mississippi, Michigan, New Jersey, and even Australia.

The Park Place Entertainment Corporation, an offshoot of

the Hilton Corporation, is the biggest gambling company in the world, with more than $4.6 billion in annual revenues and 55,000 employees. With casino interests in Canada, South Africa, Uruguay, Australia, Mississippi, Atlantic City, Reno, and Laughlin and with plans to open and manage the most lavish of California Indian casinos, its Vegas operations comprise: Bally's, Caesar's Palace, Paris, the Las Vegas Hilton, and Bugsy's old place, the Flamingo (which still commemorates its founder with a bronze plaque and a casino bar named for him).

The Mandalay Resort Group which runs casinos in Mississippi, Illinois, and Michigan, holds the prime Las Vegas properties of Mandalay Bay, the Luxor, the Excalibur, Circus Circus, and the other 50 percent of the Monte Carlo, as well as operating a half dozen other casinos in other cities of Nevada.

Taken together, these three publicly held, MBA-managed corporations are the guts and glue of the Vegas gambling industry. "Every major city in America has its central corporate business district," says historian Mike Green. "Ours just happens to be open twenty-four hours a day, has bright lights, and can be found along Las Vegas Boulevard."

Perhaps no other industry in history has in such a relatively short period so thoroughly retooled itself. From Bugsy's targeting of an elite Hollywood clientele less than sixty years ago, to a broadening outreach to the middle class in the '60s and '70s, the New Vegas now proffers an appeal to virtually every identifiable segment, niche, and demographic of the potential market.

On the booming, extreme southern end of the Strip, you "can conduct a virtual archaeological dig through the current Las Vegas customer base and yet never leave the properties of just one single company—the Mandalay Resort Group," says David Schwartz, coordinator of the Gaming Studies Research Center at UNLV.

Starting on the corner of Tropicana Avenue and running south for hundreds of yards, three MRG mega-resorts hunker cheek to cheek: the 4,000-room, 28-story Excalibur, opened in 1990; the 4,500-room Luxor, with its glass pyramid, opened in 1993; and the still expanding 3,700-room, 39-story Mandalay Bay, inaugurated in 1999. The company calls this stretch of platinum-paved real estate the Mandalay Mile.

Each hotel is owned by the same corporation, yet each blatantly targets a different social class extending an Armani appeal to some, K Mart sensibilities to others, and an odd mix to those in between. The Excalibur is definitely proletarian; you almost expect to see a rotating blue light in its lobby. The Luxor is in the middle. And the Mandalay aims for and captures an upper crust. (If that were not enough segmentation, the tony Four Seasons Hotel occupies the top five floors of the Mandalay and charges a 50 percent premium for a separate entrance that sidesteps the casino, a (smaller and quieter) pool, and more staid room furnishings.

"What's really amazing looking at those three resorts," says Schwartz "is just how willing so many people are to freely segregate themselves into different places where they feel most comfortable." Having stayed in all three of these hotels at some time or another I can personally attest to Schwartz's assertion. Enter the Mandalay and your nostrils are tickled by gardenia-scented air spicers; your heels click on buffed marble floors; every detail of décor is perfect and polished; the staff is solicitous; the rooms spacious and sumptuous. Its lagoon-like swimming pool has a sandy beach and gently swaying waves.

But for what is, in effect, only a small difference in price, the same company's Excalibur offers what must be the closest reproduction of medieval purgatory on earth. The Excalibur hotel itself is a whipped-cream-white monstrosity, topped by massive gingerbread turrets—something like a life-sized Lego castle. Arriving guests are herded into a slow, snaking check-in line, faintly reminiscent of the galling weekend wait to board Disney's Matterhorn. There's another line for the "twice knightly" dinner-jousting show. And a third line grinds lugubriously into a stark eatery featuring "Lance-A-Lotta Pizza." Dizzying brocades on the guest room rugs and drapes, and reddish-pink wallpaper imprinted to resemble . . . well . . . the bricks of a dungeon strain your brain. The room ceilings are so low that at five-foot-three I could spring up and graze them with my fingertips. At night, the powerful blue wash-lights beaming up against the walls of the hotel flood directly into the room, intentionally or otherwise, making sleep near impossible.

Yet, the Excalibur is a crass bedlam that tens of thousands eagerly check into year after year, evidently feeling too out of place at the neighboring and more humane Luxor or the posh Mandalay Bay. And they check out ready, if asked, to give rave reviews. This is the marketing genius of the phobically risk-averse corporations that now run Las Vegas.

The present is merely the past writ larger. The executives of MGM Mirage or Park Place or Mandalay Resorts could be the CEOs of any other multinational corporation. "The goal is still to make money," says Mike Green. "The difference is that once upon a time, if you owned a casino here, you might be reporting to some guys back East who might kill you if you did the wrong thing. Now you're reporting to the stockholders."

Mormons, Mobsters, and MBAs

FEW OF EVEN THE most energetic of jogging tourists rarely come this far north up Las Vegas Boulevard, a nudge past downtown to the intersection of Washington Avenue— just a few blocks short of where the city's homeless gather every morning after being turned out of their shelters. Hardly any of the millions who visit here heed the bright blue-and-yellow banner stretched along one side of Washington which reads "Come See Where Las Vegas Was Born." The ample parking lot provided by Nevada for its Old Las Vegas Mormon Fort State Historic Park is mostly, and illegally, occupied by patrons of the neighboring ball park.

Maybe that's why Nevada State Ranger E. Weaver, in her starch-crisp, olive-drab uniform seems so happy to see me when I show up one searing holiday weekend morning to the site where Vegas was founded. "Maybe we get ten people a day to come by," she says, the sun glinting off the rhinestone stars in the corner of her sunglasses.

I'm the only visitor this morning. Offering me a personal tour in return for the two-dollar admission fee, she says the first traders and explorers who came through here in the nineteenth century were drawn by its natural flowing wells and streams. Pointing to the small creek that runs under a bridge through the middle of the park, she says, "You can imagine what they must have felt when they saw this flowing water after spending weeks and miles walking through the sandy, stony desert."

When I ask if the barely damp bed of rocks in front of us is, in fact, the original creek that might have been seen by Jedediah Smith in 1826 or cartographer John C. Fremont in 1844, Ranger Weaver answers, "Sort of."

This is, after all, Las Vegas.

The three-walled, fourteen-foot-high fort, with its watch-tower and gun slits nearby, a few yards from the creek, is also a reproduction. But the thick-walled adobe building next to it which houses a meticulously organized display of photos, pictures, and primitive tools, is—in fact—the oldest building in Nevada and dates directly back to the short-lived colony established by Vegas's first white settlers, the Mormons.

In the mid-nineteenth century, what is now Las Vegas sat in the middle of a crucial but torturous path that connected the Salt Lake area with Los Angeles and was, at different times, called both the Old Spanish Trail and the Mormon Road. Mormon leader Brigham Young and his followers dreamed of establishing a string of Christian settlements along the harsh road, hoping to extend church influence and build its wealth as well as to proselytize the indigenous people that scratched out lives in the unforgiving deserts of the Southwest.

In early May of 1855, Young assembled thirty Mormons in his Utah headquarters under the leadership of William Bringhurst and sent them packing off to the south. Thirty-five days and 460 parched miles later, Bringhurst's pioneer party arrived at this site in southern Nevada and, after recovering for a few days from their arduous journey, immediately set about erecting Fort Mormon.

It wasn't just godly concerns that had motivated this adventure. Brigham Young feared that he would soon be at all-out war with the United States government over the nonconformist and vaguely communal if not communist views and practices of his acolytes. One of the Mormons' primary goals in establishing the Las Vegas settlement was, according to historians Sally Denton and Roger Morris, "to mine local metals for bullets and weapons needed for their growing resistance to U.S. rule."

Armed struggle and even a military alliance with the local Paiute was foremost on the mind of settler John Steele. The designer of the Fort and a veteran of the Mormon Battalion during the U.S.–Mexican War, Steele wrote: "We can have 1,000 brave warriors on hand in a short time to help quell the eruption that might take place."

In their sustained seach for resources they might need for eventual war with the federal government, the Mormons struck deposits of lead on nearby Mount Potosi, but the actual yields were disappointingly low and its processing was more difficult than anticipated. A dispute over the lead mining also broke out between Bringhurst and Young back in Utah. Further complicating matters, the desert soil couldn't produce enough food for the Las Vegas settlement which never numbered more than about a hundred Mormons.

The Mormons' missionary work was also a flop. Relations

with the indigenous Paiute were generally harmonious. But with food scarce in the valley, the Indians frequently pilfered the Mormon crops and cattle. To the added dismay of their Mormon saviors, the Paiute were not only indulgently tolerant of some egregious gender-bending, but by some accounts, they were also, well, degenerate gamblers. The authors of the classic Vegas exposé, *The Green Felt Jungle,* described the Paiute as spending vast hours of the day "rolling bones and colored sticks in the brown sand, the true ancestors of the modern Vegas."

Only two years after founding their settlement, the original Las Vegas Mormons crapped out. Most returned to Utah, while some followed Bringhurst down the road to the settlement in San Bernardino, California. But the Mormons had imprinted a lasting legacy—Nevada, and most certainly Las Vegas, would be built by others like them: the ostracized, the outcasts, the oddballs, the outlaws, just about everybody and anybody who didn't easily fit into a growing America.

While the original attempt to settle the southern Nevada valley around Las Vegas collapsed, other parts of the state boomed as another wave of gamblers and speculators poured in from across the nation—this time not as polygamous missionaries but rather in the guise of prospectors and miners. As they swung their picks and axes digging for fortune in what became the world-famous Comstock Lode, this new crop of American self-exiles would sing:

What Was Your Name in the States?
Oh, what was your name in the States?
Was it Thompson, or Johnson, or Bates?
Did you murder your wife and fly for your life?
Say, what was your name in the States?

The abandoned Fort Mormon, meanwhile, became a private ranch and Las Vegas languished as a fairly unremarkable and barely noticed watering hole for dusty travelers. Not until the turn of the century, when Montana copper baron and Senator William Clark completed his San Pedro, Los Angeles & Salt Lake line did Las Vegas finally wind up on the map.

The imperious Clark, who had once tried to buy off the entire Montana legislature, had raced the rival Union Pacific and then eventually partnered with it to finish the rail line which would shorten the route from his home-state copper mines to the California ports by hundreds of miles.

To water his locomotives, Clark's railroad snapped up the water rights from the Las Vegas Ranch which had supplanted Fort Mormon, as well as most of the land around it (Clark purchased the Ranch for fifty-five-thousand dollars in 1902). Around the single-car rail depot he established, dozens and eventually hundreds of rail workers lived in wood-framed tents, beginning the transformation of Las Vegas into a typical western roundhouse town.

On the morning of May 15, 1905, more than a thousand people poured out under a furnace-like sun for the auction that would parcel out Clark's land and establish the town site he had planned with prime "downtown" lots going for eight hundred dollars or more. With that land rush, Las Vegas was formally born.

From its inception, Vegas served to satisfy the urges of travelers and transients. As Clark's locomotives would pull in for three hours of loading and unloading at the depot, sun-baked passengers would disembark and lustily sample the otherwise forbidden pleasures of booze, poker, and sex from among the offerings of what a few decades later would became a full-blown red light district in the heart of the fledgling downtown. Block 16, as it was called, was a two-street stretch that permitted the sale of alcohol and was recalled recently in the *Las Vegas Mercury* by Gregory Crosby who wrote that it featured "in almost embryonic form, the first plea-suredome in a city destined to be the pleasuredome of the Western world, as initially ramshackle saloons crowded into the small place." As early as 1906 gambling and prostitution—both suppos-edly illegal—flowed freely along with the liquor, and the back rooms and second floors of the gritty sawdust-floored saloons beck-oned with rows of hot-sheet prostitution "cribs."

The swank Arizona Club bloomed alongside the lesser Double O, Star and Gem saloons and from its earliest railroad depot days, Block 16 flourished as a jumping, anything-goes nightspot until the U.S. military—worried about the welfare and piety of the thousands of its wartime troops stationed in and around Vegas—effectively shut it down in 1942. But by then, Vegas vice had already begun to move out of the shadows and toward the light of the just-emerging Strip—that long stretch of highway connecting, eventually, with Los Angeles.

The evolution of the Strip and its Sin City incarnation is owed to a rapid-fire concatenation of events—a confluence so fortuitous and uncanny that Las Vegas, which in the late 1920s had a pop-ulation of barely a few thousand, began to boom precisely as the rest of the country floundered in the Great Depression.

There was hardly anything certain about this outcome. Vegas's very survival was, at first, a close call. After a bitter strike five years earlier, in 1927, Bill Clark's railroad moved much of its operations out of Vegas and up-line to the desolate desert post of Caliente. Vegas was left reeling, and teetered on anonymity and abandonment.

But then came an unprecedented streak of luck. First, the

tight corset that the Progressive era strapped on American public and private morality was substantially loosened by the post-World War I partying of the Roaring Twenties.

Then, also in 1927, the Nevada state legislature, with an uncannily clever eye on attracting tourists, established the then-unheard-of six-week quickie divorce. While this law—by far the most liberal in the nation at that time—primarily boosted the fortunes of Reno, the "Biggest Little City in the World," it also helped buoy the fledgling Las Vegas.

A year later, after tedious and drawn-out negotiations among the southwestern states and the federal government, the U.S. Congress finally approved the Boulder Dam project. The erection of the world's largest dam and Roosevelt's New Deal would open the financial sluice gates allowing some seventy million dollars in federal funds to gush into the region over the next decade. Water and electricity would be abundant as sunshine. Meanwhile, the thousands of laborers who came to build the dam were mostly penned up and kept isolated from liquor (and unions) in the town of Boulder—to this day the only dry city in Nevada. Neighboring Las Vegas with its bawdy Block 16, just a few miles down the road, immediately became their weekend Mecca.

State legislators were also delighted by the thousands—the hundreds of thousands—of tourists trying out their new highway-worthy cars who began to putter into southern Nevada to goggle at the rising dam. Desperate to keep the tourist flow steady even after the dam would be built, Las Vegas commercial interests, Reno businessmen and, naturally enough, illegal gamblers (including, it was later discovered, Al Capone) pressured the Nevada legislature to re-legalize gambling—which had been banned by the Progressives in 1913.

When Nevada political boss George Wingfield cast his lot

with the pro-gambling forces in February 1931, Nevada green-lighted legal casinos—a fact that was hardly lost on attentive gamblers and gangsters across America. "Nevada, from the early days of mining, was always one way or another a company state," says Michael Green. "In 1931 we merely changed companies."

Indeed, the wholesale legalization of casino gambling had flung wide open the doors for investment in a new and highly lucrative American industry. That a whole new class of entrepreneurs would immediately rush forward to exploit this opportunity should surprise no one. It was merely different (to be polite) nontraditional investors who were willing to bankroll such a stigmatized industry—organized crime.

Almost overnight, the sawdust saloons in the downtown Block 16 area applied for gambling licenses. And then on July 4, 1931, a handful of miles south on the dark and virtually bare Highway 91, known as the Los Angeles Freeway, just outside of the Las Vegas city limits, Frank Detra, an alleged associate of Chicago syndicate boss Al Capone, opened up his Pair-O-Dice Club to the public, offering Italian dinners, live music, primitive air conditioning and legal gambling to anyone who walked through the door. And by opening up what was essentially little more than a roadhouse, Detra had, unknowingly, founded the Las Vegas Strip.

After a number of false starts, name changes, and snags with Prohibition laws, the Pair O'Dice tavern was bought in 1939 by Guy McAfee, a corrupt L.A.P.D. vice commander and one of southern California's most notorious gamblers. Contrary to the myth popularized by the film *Bugsy,* mobster Benjamin Siegel was not the original Strip visionary, nor even the man who first used the term. Credit that to McAfee. Heaven only knows what was in that ex-cop's head when he told friends that the desolate and unpopulated stretch of highway where his small club stood not only reminded him of the bustling Sunset Strip back home in Hollywood, crammed with nightclubs and bars, but one day would rival and even surpass it.

According to former State Historical Society curator Frank Wright, "In the 1930s the Vegas Chamber of Commerce cast Las Vegas as an Old West, frontier town. As a cowboy town. But that was just a marketing gimmick. In reality, Las Vegas was dominated from the outset by sophisticated, urban gamblers from across the country. But primarily from L. A."

In 1938, when reform-minded Los Angeles mayor Fletcher Bowron took office and shut down the local card rooms, clandestine casinos, and the fleet of gambling ships that had bobbed in the waters from Santa Monica to Catalina Island, he only accelerated the underworld exodus toward Nevada.

Bugsy Siegel had first come to Vegas in 1941 as a West Coast envoy of Meyer Lansky, charged with the mission of extending mob control over the local racing wire. That accomplished, Siegel started investing in downtown Vegas casinos around the old Block 16. In one short period he bought and sold the El Cortez gambling hall which still stands today on Fremont Street.

The same year that Bugsy came out to Vegas, the first two direct ancestors of today's mega-casinos, the full-service gambling resorts El Rancho Vegas and the Last Frontier, blossomed on the Strip. As a child I stayed in both hotels and remember them clearly as ornate, Western-themed operations—the Frontier had even reconstructed an entire pioneer village on its grounds. Bugsy also visited these two inaugural properties and they inspired him to move in and take over construction of the Strip's third resort, the Flamingo.

Bugsy can be credited in two crucial ways. He effectively led the rush of mob investment capital into Las Vegas. And he consciously decided to break with the cowboy themes of the first resorts. He might not have envisioned the Strip, per se. But Bugsy Siegel was certainly the intellectual godfather and spiritual architect of the transformation of Las Vegas into Sin City. Historian Rothman argues that Bugsy conceived "the complicated relationship between gaming and status that would make the Flamingo Hotel and Casino a world-class destination resort. Siegel transformed Las Vegas from a western, institution-free center of vice into a world-renowned spectacle of gambling, entertainment, and fun by melding the themes of Monte Carlo, Miami Beach, and Havana with the resort-like character of the clubs that preceded the Flamingo on Highway 91 south of town on the road to Los Angeles."

For all his efforts, and mostly for gross cost overruns at the Flamingo (Bugsy had insisted on individual sewer lines from each guest room), Siegel was assassinated in his Beverly Hills mansion by his more powerful partners in 1947.

But when Moe Dalitz and his gangster partners from Cleveland opened the Desert Inn three years later, mob financing of the burgeoning resort city was firmly established. Using the pooled retirement funds of hardworking blue-collar truck drivers and warehouse workers across America, Dalitz helped direct the flow of Teamster millions into the rat-a-tat opening of the Sands, the Hacienda, the Stardust, the Tropicana, and later Caesar's Palace, the original Aladdin, and the Landmark.

The same year that Dalitz and his front man, Wilbur Clark, were opening the D.I., the crusading and colorful Tennessee Senator Estes Kefauver launched his anti-racketeering crusade and, unwittingly, fueled the informal convening of a nationwide gangster diaspora in Las Vegas, a city which was quickly rising as the gambling capital of the Western world.

Kenny Franks, who arrived at the Desert Inn as a young and well connected dealer in 1957, today remembers those days in Vegas as a time when he'd constantly bump into other casino workers and managers from "fraternal organizations" from across the nation. "A lot of the dealers that opened the D.I. . . . were all part of the Cleveland-Newport-Kentucky-Cincinnati move," he says. "Some came from the old Beverly Hills Club. There were also guys who came from all the gambling places around Toledo and Steubenville. All these guys were already pros by the time they hit Vegas."

Fidel Castro also did his part to assure Las Vegas's preeminence in hemispheric vice when his 1959 socialist revolution shuttered Havana's notorious casinos and bordellos. As outside gangster funding and influence washed through Vegas, whatever there was of an indigenous Nevada political, economic, and even social elite weren't complaining, at least not publicly. Nor were they intimidated. Grateful and solicitous might be better descriptors. They were more than ready, as Hal Rothman says, to be "colonized" by L.A. mobsters and their financial sugar daddies so long as it guaranteed their own prosperity.

The mobsters, in turn, took few pains to mask their control of the city. "Moe Dalitz was in the D.I. casino all the time," Kenny Franks remembers. "He was a well-spoken guy who unlike others didn't talk out of the corner of his mouth. He'd stand there often in a tuxedo and you knew he was the guy you eventually went to solve any problem. His word was absolutely final. But he wore a suit—not a machine gun."

Once again, a railroad figures in the next phase of Vegas' development. Billionaire Howard Hughes arrived in his beloved Las Vegas by cover of darkness in the wee hours of Thanksgiving Day in 1966 when a sealed train delivered him on a stretcher at a depot on the northern edge of town. As soon as the ailing Hughes was unloaded he was secretly rushed to and then sealed off again on the top floor of the Desert Inn. Hughes might have arrived in Vegas much the same way (except for the stretcher) as V. I. Lenin once covertly rolled into Russia during World War I. But Hughes, contrary to myth, led no revolt that toppled the mafia in Vegas. Instead, when he finally emerged from his hole-up in the D.I. four years later, he would leave a legacy as a sort of modern-day reverse-Kerensky, serving as a transitional figure that eventually unleashed a full-blown revolution—in this case, the corporate capitalist revolution that mightily rules Vegas today.

Those tumultuous four years of Hughes's initial ascendance are rife with lore and legend. Some say Hughes may never have been here, as virtually no one ever saw him. There are also the wonderful, and mostly true, stories that he bought the local TV station just so, in those days before VCRs, he could watch his favorite Hollywood movies in the middle of the night. Or that after he bought the Silver Slipper casino, he ordered an end to the rotation of the trademark mirror-covered shoe on the roof, as the light it reflected disturbingly bounced into his suite next door at the D.I.

Yet, some hard facts are undisputed. Shortly after Hughes arrived at the D.I., Moe Dalitz gingerly but directly asked him to leave and make room for the high-stakes players that the hotel traditionally housed in the top-floor suites which were occupied by the eccentric billionaire and his entourage. Hughes countered the eviction request by forking over thirteen million dollars to buy the D.I., kicking off his rise to power in Vegas.

In whirlwind fashion, Hughes unpocketed tens of millions

more and snapped up the Sands, the Frontier, the Castaways, the Landmark, Harold's Club in Reno, the Silver Slipper, the Vegas affiliate of CBS, and some big chunks of desert land northwest of downtown Vegas. Soon controlling a third of gambling income on the Strip, Hughes became Nevada's largest employer and biggest landowner and went on to make a number of unsuccessful bids to take over other casinos, TV stations, and even the leading local daily newspaper.

But to say Hughes simply bought out the mob is an oversimplification. The middle-management of the casinos he took over, in most cases, stayed on and the transition to corporate control was completed only in the early 1980s. Historian Michael Green jokes that "Hughes might have been the biggest pigeon that ever flew into Vegas. He wanted Mormons in charge of his casinos. And while Mormons may be honest, they don't know much about gambling. So the guys in the count rooms and casino pits were the same as always and so was the skimming, the corruption—all the same old stuff went on for quite some time."

Yet, Hughes's Vegas predominance neatly coincided with what were the natural limits of underworld funding. Las Vegas in the late '60s and early '70s was growing too fast and was starting to require financing beyond the means of the old mob syndicates. Institutionalized gambling was becoming far too rich a field to be left to mere gangsters.

The cleaned-up image that Hughes projected on Vegas spurred an alliance comprised of conservative Governor Paul Laxalt, the Hilton Corporation, and other business interests, to pass the Corporate Gaming Act of 1967, and then a strengthened version of it two years later. Nevada law, prior to the Act, had pretty much guaranteed mob control over gambling by insisting that every stockholder in a casino operation be licensed by the state. Any corporation planning to run a casino would, theoretically, have to seek a gambling license for each and every one of its thousands of stockholders.

But the Gaming Act paved the way for Wall Street to move in, requiring only a few top executives of any casino corporation to be cleared by state gambling regulators.

The capitalist revolution soon got formally underway and its first beachhead was won as soon as 1970 when the Hilton corporation bought the Flamingo and the sprawling International Hotel and Casino from entrepreneur Kirk Kerkorian. Corporate America could sense the profit frenzy about to ensue. Things were so profitable, in fact, that in 1976, the Hilton corporation, which owned a total of 163 hotels worldwide, derived a whopping 43 percent of its gross revenues from just its two Vegas holdings. The Ramada corporation and even the squeaky clean Holiday Inn began buying into Vegas. In modern America, how could the heirs and minions of Meyer Lansky compete with a corporation that had a Doris Day image?

"In this climate, organized crime suddenly became financially obsolete," says Rothman. "In an instant, the passage of the revised Corporate Gaming Act redistributed power in Las Vegas away from the Teamsters and toward Wall Street."

By the late '80s and early '90s Steve Wynn would take Vegas development to an even higher level, seeking and achieving access to the very broadest sources of modern capitalist funding—roaring rivers of cash unimaginable to the likes of a Bugsy Siegel or Meyer Lansky.

Born to a family dominated by a father that was an incurable gambler and bingo operator, Wynn personified the bridge between the old Vegas and its newest incarnation that he would spawn. Wynn came to Vegas in 1967 after inheriting his father's

East Coast bingo operation and for a lowball price bought a small piece of the Frontier Hotel. While producing entertainment acts, he developed a bond with the older E. Parry Thomas whose Valley Bank had served as the conduit for hundreds of millions in Teamster Central States Pension funding for mob-run casinos. Wynn got richer off some quick land deals that Thomas helped engineer and by 1973, at only age thirty-one, again with the old banker's assistance, Wynn took over the lackluster downtown Golden Nugget casino. One of his first acts was to fire more than 150 crooked employees that had made the place a notorious tourist shake-down joint. An old 1940s gambling saloon with no hotel rooms, the Nugget would eventually be transformed by Wynn into downtown's glimmering jewel. He added on a four-star hotel and enlisted none other than Frank Sinatra to come perform downtown, something no other big name entertainer would previously deign to do. More startling to his stunned competitors, Wynn convinced Sinatra to star in an expensive and highly effective national TV advertising campaign promoting the upgraded Nugget. (Wynn brilliantly accepted a self-denigrating role in his own TV spots, allowing Old Blue Eyes to call him "kid" and order him to find some extra towels.)

But along the way to making the once-tarnished Nugget shine, Wynn made a fortuitous friendship and business partnership that would shake Las Vegas and all of the gambling world to its foundations. In putting together the financing for an Atlantic City twin of the Nugget in the late '70s, Wynn turned to Michael Milken, the junk-bond specialist from Drexel Burnham Lambert Inc. who conjured up $160 million for the project. After starting out as the student of Teamster ally Thomas and ending up as partners with the icon of '80s, Gordon

Gekko-like capitalism Mike Milken, Wynn cemented the historic link between the oldest of Vegas's traditions and its still unforeseen future.

It may have been unforseen by many, but not by the coldly calculating Milken. "In the late seventies I'd take money managers and pension fund people into the casinos and show them that it wasn't a gambling business," Milken is quoted as saying in John L. Smith's biography of Wynn, *Running Scared.* "It was a business that was built on the laws of probability and statistics." In the mid-'80s, when Wynn's conception of a flamboyant Strip mega-resort was, indeed, still a mirage, he knew he could turn to Milken and his junk-bond financing to make it a reality. "No Milken, no Mirage," is how Wynn is repeatedly quoted by biographer Smith.

In 1989 Wynn opened his spectacular Mirage on the mid-Strip, with a price tag of $630 million—a mind-boggling half-billion dollars more than had ever been sunk into a Vegas property. Just to cover his debt service, Wynn had to clear one million dollars a day in his new casino—an impossible feat to many insiders who were certain—and some even anxious—he would fail. Instead, the flashy Mirage gambling floor was soon earning twice that figure, taking in forty million dollars the first month. The property posted a profit of nearly forty-five million dollars in its first quarter as it vacuumed up clients and business from the rest of the Strip properties that couldn't compete with its startling grandeur. Immediately next door, the venerable and luxurious Caesar's Palace took a staggering body blow as it was dethroned as the Strip's presiding property.

The Mirage set new, almost unthinkable, benchmarks in Vegas resort marketing, turning every corner of the property—not just the casino—into a money-minting machine. Historic giveaway room rates began to cede to the Mirage policy of charging $350 or more a night on premium weekends. The burbling volcano, the indoor rain forest, the dolphin habitat, the rare white tigers, the ultra-posh private quarters for high-rollers, and the bombastic nightly magic show of Siegfried and Roy, whose act—a dozen years later—continues to attract one-hundred-dollar-a-seat full houses, provided a level of dazzling spectacle that even Vegas couldn't previously imagine.

A year after the Mirage opened, Mike Milken crashed as he plead to insider trading charges. But the die had already been cast. The screaming success of Steve Wynn's Mirage set off the New Vegas revolution that in the space of barely ten years radically remade Sin City, more than doubling its population, almost doubling the number of its hotel rooms, and sprouting construction cranes like the spines on the back of a roused porcupine. As the national economy sagged in the midst of the recession that would cost George H. W. Bush the presidency in 1992, thousands of job-hungry American families, like a prolonged wave of new Oakies, poured into Vegas and found new livelihoods in the mobile trailers the casinos and construction companies set up along the Strip as hiring offices. The already hefty Culinary Workers Local 226 swelled into one of the most powerful unions in the country as, overnight, downsized and displaced Rust Belt meat-packers and textile machine operators retooled themselves in the Nevada desert as hotel cooks and maids, if not construction drywallers and carpenters or casino craps dealers and parking valets.

The year after the Mirage debuted, the longer-established Circus Circus Enterprises opened the second, more blue-collar, mega resort on the Strip, the Excalibur. In 1993 alone Wynn opened his Treasure Island, as the exotic Luxor, also owned by

Circus Circus, opened farther south down the Strip. Kirk Kerkorian upped the ante when, in the same year, he inaugurated his gargantuan-sized nine-hundred-million-dollar MGM Grand across the street from the glass pyramid. In 1998 Wynn trumped everyone again with his elegant, decidedly upscale $1.2 billion Bellagio, a sprawling evocation of Italy's northern Lake District, featuring dancing fountains, a battery of gourmet restaurants, a plush caviar bar, and a three-hundred-million-dollar fine art collection. Only months later, the Mandalay Bay opened its doors and awed it customers with what appeared to be a an even ritzier redux of the Mirage.

As other corporations moved into Vegas and new ones were formed, in part as Wynn sold off his holdings in 2000 (though he would soon enough reappear on the Strip with his Le Reve project), the transition of Las Vegas from Sin City to Disney-in-the-desert, the shift from the era of "mobsters and mavericks to MBAs" as UNLV's Bo Bernhard puts it, was fully completed. The rum-running gunboats of the mob had been swamped and sunk by the veritable nuclear-missile cruisers of corporate capital. The world of the Five Families could hardly compete against the global muscle of the Big Board.

Part Two

January–June 2003

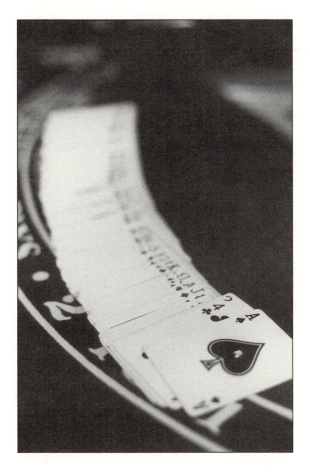

The Naked and the Red

S THE MIRRORED DISCO ball cranks and splotches of purplish black-light reflect off the three polished chrome dance poles, the live DJ in the back of the room puts his mouth right on his mike and yells out, "And now . . . give it up for Colette!"

It's a lazy Wednesday afternoon in the near empty Déjà Vu Showgirls "gentlemen's club." No more than a half dozen patrons slouch in their seats sipping their drinks—strictly sodas and juices. This is an all-nude club and unlike the less explicit topless bars, no alcohol is permitted here. Even inside the private and darkened Champagne Room, the basic two-hundred-dollar rate will only get you a magnum bottle of carbonated grape juice for your half-hour stay.

This afternoon the crowd is a more modest crew that has paid a flat twenty-dollar cover charge each which allows them to sit at a table or right at the edge of the stage for as long as they desire, and ogle the never-ending, around-the-clock, we're-open-on-holidays parade of nude dancers.

A thousand-decibel techno rendition of "Sex on Wheels" rattles the speakers and the floor as the just-announced Colette, a tall and lanky brunette, wearing only white boots, a pink G-string around her bottom and a white chiffon handkerchief around her neck struts into the spotlight. Within seconds she is down on the stage floor, teasing the two guys seated at the foot of the stage with her ample breasts, and five dollar tips begin trickling forth. She briefly exits offstage as the music shifts and then reappears, now shed of her G-string and handkerchief and stripped down only to her boots. She squats on her knees on the elevated stage floor and leans backward giving the room a full-on view between her legs. The guys in front, a foot from her exposed crotch, respond by anteing up with more flashes of green.

When her cyclical seven-minute-per-hour stint on stage ends, Colette slowly walks down the aisles between the tables on the showroom floor, trolling for lap-dance solicitations. For twenty dollars plus a tip, Colette, or any of the other dancers here, will take you into a side room, sit you down in a chair and gyrate, groan, and writhe buck naked on your lap for precisely four minutes. "The idea is that about three-and-a-half minutes into it, you take it up a notch, getting the guy really worked up," Colette tells me, detailing her commercial strategy. "Then right before the time is up, I stick my mouth right in the guy's ear and whisper 'You want another one, honey?' If you're doing well, you get 'em to go three, four dances right in a row and you pick up a hundred bucks or so. Some guys string out six or seven dances."

The customer can also pay a premium and have the dance on a

couch or on a reclining lounge. For the more discriminating, and the more financially endowed, there are also themed rooms available: the Dungeon, the Shower, and that booze-free Champagne Room. "It's sixty bucks minimum if I have to get wet with them," Colette says of the Shower option. But business is slow this hour and she has no comers.

When Colette is offstage her name is Andrea Lee Hackett—though some call her the Norma Rae of Las Vegas. For when she's not bumping and grinding, she's out leafleting and circulating petitions or doing talk-radio interviews. I've come to see her precisely because over the last few months her name keeps popping up in the local papers as the feisty founding president of the Las Vegas Dancers Alliance—a fledgling movement that is organizing and pitting this city's thousands of strippers and nude dancers into a direct confrontation with local government and indirectly with the corporate gambling interests that dominate Vegas's political life. A specter haunts the Las Vegas Strip—unionized strippers.

This colorful episode of open class-warfare erupted last summer when the Clark County commissioners voted five to one to heavily regulate the couple of dozen dance clubs that operate around the Strip and that draw huge numbers of enthusiastic conventioneers and tourists.

Like a Church Lady skit right off of *Saturday Night Live,* in the summer of 2002 the county commissioners took a hands-on approach—no pun intended—defining by ordinance that which would now make a lap dance legal or illegal. After what some described as a Keystone Cops-like eighteen month undercover investigation by the Metro police, officials concluded that too much of the dancing had blurred into prostitution and that it was now time to stamp it out, even in Sin City. By the standards of the newly passed ordinance, a dancer would no longer be permitted to sit on a customer's genital area—i.e. his lap—more or less rendering the very essence of the dance impotent. Nor could dancers directly solicit tips. Cameras would be installed in all private dance rooms and could be centrally monitored in a control room open, at will, to law enforcement. And, until pressure from Andrea's group and others forced a revision, the time-honored frat-boy tradition of stuffing tips directly into undulating G-strings was also verboten.

"This was a declaration of war. In short, they were outlawing lap dancing," Andrea says to me the next afternoon while sipping coffee at a Starbucks and unpacking a thick file of organizational battle charts, news clippings, and Excel printouts she has brought along. She vows not to only organize the city's dancers, but eventually to unionize them. "They wanted a fight," she says of the county politicians. "And now I'm going to give it to them."

At first blush, the Clark County lap-dance ordinance had no logic, to say the least. Clubs operating inside the Vegas city limits—mostly around downtown—faced no such restriction. Further, open the *Las Vegas Yellow Pages* and you'll swim through a mind-boggling hundred pages or more of ads from "entertainer" services including full-page displays for "Full Service Casino House Girls . . . Full Service Barely Eighteen . . . Barely Legal College Cheerleaders. . . . Full Service Freelance Girls," and so on. Prostitution, while permitted in nearby counties, is illegal in the Las Vegas area. But everyone knows that for a price the outcall ladies will do anything asked of them and few of these "dancers" have spent much time with the Joffrey. Women who work for these services describe them as little more than pimping agencies. They charge the client's credit card—promising him nothing illegal—a fee of about $150, none of which goes to the women. Once the date is made, the woman directly negotiates an additional fee for "full service" which is wholly hers, along with all the attendant risks. Regulating lap dancing, then, was hardly going to stamp out the Vegas hooker trade. If anything, it would divert spurned lap-dance clients directly toward prostitutes. More absurd, the new law banned minors—the girls between the age of eighteen and twenty-one—from dancing in the alcohol-free all-nude clubs, forcing many of them to take up working in the booze-laden topless-only bars.

Andrea, forty-nine years old and looking at least a decade younger, uses her exquisitely manicured nails to dig into her smokes, lights one up, exhales, and then, her hoarse voice sounding a bit like that of a think-tank economist, says to me, "This is life in the post-9/11 economic environment. It's all about the corporations shifting their revenue and profit streams away from gaming. It's all about the casinos wanting to get rid of the competition."

But why would the mighty casinos be threatened by places like the Déjà Vu where Andrea dances? It's enough to take a cruise down the once-aptly named Industrial Road to crash right into the answer. The gritty thoroughfare that runs parallel and behind glittering Las Vegas Boulevard is the literal ass-end of the Strip, pocked with dingy car parts stores and grimy machine shops. But there's also the Elvis-a-Rama Museum with its twice daily live impersonator show and, much more importantly, a dozen or more clubs like the Déjà Vu. Many of them much more glorious, as well. On any weekend night, look out for the bumper-to-bumper pileups as taxis, limos, and private cars elbow each other out to slip into the dance-club parking lots. One local observer averred that "a million" lap dances a year are performed by the twenty-five thousand or so licensed dancers in Clark County. And a minimum of asking around reveals that lap dancing is to Vegas what porn is to the Internet—its dirty little secret, one of its principal but unspoken attractions.

But not so covert anymore. Try out this math: the recently opened Sapphire, just up the street from the Déjà Vu, with multiple dance stages, marble floors, hi-tech plasma screens, plush carpets, and an upscale atmosphere, weighed in with a staggering thirty-million-dollar price tag. A row of thirteen top-ticket skyboxes line the upper reaches of the club, allowing big spenders a yawning view of the 2,000 or more customers and 250 or more near-naked dancers that can flood the floor on a busy night. It's sprawling 71,000-square-foot club gobbles up 7 acres of prime real estate. Nearby sits the 25,000 square foot Jaguars Club. Later, this year, another thirty-million-dollar, ultra-luxurious dance club, Treasures, is to open in the same neighborhood.

The casinos, which have always strained to keep their customers bottled up and captive to the tables and slots, cannot be but panicked and horror-stricken over the flood of visitors and cash flowing toward the dance clubs. Andrea's theory that the top-line casinos, barred by state regulation law from mixing gambling with all-nude or lap dancing, are calling in their chips with local politicians to put the squeeze on the swelling club scene is perfectly plausible.

The tussle also reflects the profound and ongoing identity crisis that afflicts the Vegas establishment—to be or not to be Sin City. Wrapped up in that struggle are all the inherent contradictions of what sociologist David Dickens calls "a highly managed environment of commercialized vice, of commodified sleaze." For a few years in the early '90s, as the post-Mirage mega-resorts snapped open, the city marketed itself as a "family destination resort."

Bring along the kiddies, this place is also for them. At the time, the Mirage's chief flack, Alan Feldman told me that "we have to find a new public for Las Vegas, and the biggest untapped pool are those people who won't travel without their kids. So we're giving a little something for the kids to do, too. What we are really after is what Disney said. He's not after the kids, but rather the kids inside of all of us." The kid, and his piggy bank and penny jar, he might have added.

Notwithstanding Feldman's noble thoughts, the family resort idea soon flopped "just as soon as the casinos figured out that kids don't really gamble very much," as one wag quipped. You knew this phase was way over when the MGM Grand dismantled the radically ignored amusement park it had built behind its hotel. It seems that Vegas marketers are still not quite sure how to sell their product nowadays, coming up with an often lumpy blend you might call Nice Vice.

Maybe the *most* disingenuous aspect of Las Vegas today is witnessed driving down the Strip and seeing the piercingly lit sign of Caesar's Palace turn red-white-and-blue and announce "One Nation Under God." Or the MGM with its own tricolored illuminated billboard stating "United We Stand." You just know that nobody behind those signs cares anything about such high-minded themes of international affairs. Much more convincing is how Vegas promotion has returned to rely more and more on more mundane affairs, namely, on affairs of the flesh, on plain-old-fashioned sex—especially after the 9/11 terrorist attacks put the first serious crimp in business in decades.

Millions are currently being spent by the Las Vegas Convention and Visitors Authority on a highly suggestive TV ad campaign reminding the panting viewer that "What Happens Here, Stays Here." One of the higly produced spots features a writhing, purring woman trying to seduce her limousine driver. Another ad in the series stars a more staid female convention-goer leaving a quickie marriage chapel with her much younger Latin lover, and giving him one last kiss and lascivious sniff before—ostensibly—boarding a plane back home to her routine *Ozzie and Harriet* everyday life. Billboards along the Vegas strip—when not flashing jingoistic bumper sticker slogans—are back to mostly peddling sex and skin. One set of Strip billboards features a zipper and announces "Sin City Has Found Its Soul."

Speaking to the Associated Press about their planned La Reve which will supplant the old Desert Inn, Steve Wynn's wife and partner, Elaine Wynn, confirmed the new trend. "We know the club scene is very desirable for Las Vegas visitors," she said. "We intend to offer our guests alternatives that we hope will satisfy their desires." This from the entreprenuerial family that first brought "family values" to Vegas marketing barely a decade ago.

In direct competition with the dance clubs, the flashy X-Generation hangout casino, the Palms, recently inaugurated a group of "bachelor party" guest rooms replete with chrome poles for in-room dancers and a new *nighttime* swimming suit-bash at its pool. The Paris Hotel and Casino opened the new Risqué club featuring burlesque dancers decked out in boas. The MGM pushes a girlie show called "La Femme" and has recently opened the $7 million Tabú lounge where table service costs a minimum $225. Dress attire is required but shots of raw tequila are also fired out from pumps buried in the cleavage of well-endowed cocktail waitresses. At the Rio, the Bikini Bar is now open for business and so on down a long and growing list of turns toward more sexually explicit entertainment. Even the pretentiously arty Cirque Du Soleil is set to open its new fifteen-million-dollar "Zumanity" show at the New York New York resort, which will highlight a "provocative exhibition of human sensuality, arousal, and eroticism." Couples are encouraged to buy a joint $195 ticket on what are being called Love Seats and Duo Sofas from which they can view the show, which will include, according to the *New York Times,* "a sadomasochistic prison scenario, a drag queen who channels Billie Holiday, and couplings in configurations across the sexual range." The lead role in the show has been won by Joey Arias, a celebrated fixture of the New York drag queen scene. Not exactly kiddie fare.

Coming full circle from the days of family values, the Treasure Island casino's thrice-nightly open air pirate battle—a shameless but bigger scale knockoff of Disney's legendary Pirates of the Caribbean ride—was retooled for a rechristening in the fall of 2003. The sword-slinging swashbucklers are to be replaced by scantily-clad "sirens" who will rappel down from the topmasts. The juvenile-sounding name of the hotel is being officially shortened to a simple and engimatic "T.I." How far off can we be from spicing up the tired and wholesome volcano show next door at the Mirage with the simulated sacrifice of buxom and leggy virgins?

Andrea's now on her fourth or fifth cigarette as she explains how she founded the Las Vegas Dancers Alliance last summer, just as the fight over the lap dance ordinance was cresting. In short order, she helped pack the County Commission hearing room with three hundred outraged dancers and their supporters. She jumpstarted a hard-hitting media lobbying campaign. The LVDA has inserted a network of "club reps," clandestine shop stewards, in about two-thirds of the dance clubs. Monthly meetings at the local library and outreach leafleting have brought in more than five hundred memberships.

She's also affiliated the LVDA with the left-of-center Progressive Leadership Alliance of Nevada (PLAN), which includes groups like the Sierra Club and the NAACP. "Andrea's got the energy of ten organizers and the skills to go along with it," PLAN's Southern Nevada director Paul Brown had already told me before I met her. She'd also built a working relationship with the local American Civil Liberties Union.

"The fight isn't just against the County, it's also against the club owners," she says. She admits that when times are good, like during the salad days of the '90s stock market boom, a capable dancer might have pocketed two or three thousand dollars a week. With the national economy now sputtering, most dancers, herself included, are down to a third or less of those earnings. "And we are exploited by everybody," she says. Vegas dancers are not employees of the clubs, but rather "independent contractors," bereft of benefits and health insurance. It's they who pay the owners for the "right" to perform, essentially renting space on the floor at the rate of seventy dollars or more per shift. They also have to split the fees they take in for the individual lap dances, sometimes at a fifty-fifty ratio. "At this rate, you're not making any money until you've done your seventh dance. And nowadays, you might not get seven dances in a night," she says. Then there's the payoffs to bouncers, the DJs, sometimes even the parking valets. Her dream—really her determined quest, way beyond fighting the lap dance ordinance—is to win legal employee status for the dancers and enroll them in a fighting union. She's already been talking to the Teamsters.

As the afternoon began to fade to dusk, Andrea pulls out a copy of a pamphlet billing itself as the "first ever" Dancer's Voter Guide, something her group circulated during the fall 2002 elections. And then she tells me she's working to complete her own "Politics of Dancing" educational course—designed, she says, to offer a quick political education to the average apolitical 19-year-old nude dancer. She's already written a primer, a 7,500-word draft she hands me.

I begin reading through it and am immediately taken by its sophistication and clarity. Tightly written and well-argued, it delivers a strong ideological punch, a sweeping left hook. Her draft concludes saying she hopes her work can "help solidify the great natural allies of the American left and begin to heal the wounds inflicted by our natural enemies on the right . . . The first basic facts to remember are these: There are far less rich people than poor people. And the rich generally want things to stay the way they are. The poor, by their very nature, want things to change, hopefully for the better."

I put down the pamphlet a bit stunned, hardly expecting to find whiffs of Wobbly unionism flickering in the boobie-bars of Vegas. I also have to confront my own prejudices and ask myself why I'm so surprised to find a nude dancer as politically passionate, as determined, and as damn articulate as Andrea. After all, there are plenty of women working their way through grad school dealing cards in the casinos or shaking their bottoms in the clubs. But it all still seems with Andrea, somehow, a bit off.

"I'm sorry to patronize you," I venture. "But let me put it this way: Who are you really? Where'd you pick all this up? Surely not working in dance clubs?"

"No," Andrea answers. "No. This isn't exactly new to me. I worked for seventeen years for the Boeing Corporation. All of those years in the union. And later the company asked me to help them organize their middle management as a consultant. That's where I learned a lot of these skills."

"Boeing? In Seattle? The only union I know there is the

Machinists. What were you, a lathe operator?" I ask, conjuring up images of Rosie the Riveter.

Andrea pauses a moment, then shakes her head back with a big smile. "Yeah, that's right. I was in the Machinists union. Built scaffolds, worked some machinery, did some painting. I worked seventeen years on the shop floor—and then—and then—in 1995 after I came back from my sex change operation, well, the guys on the floor just didn't see me the old way and I was sent upstairs. Must have been my new breasts bulging through my shirt."

And then she breaks out laughing loudly in unison with me. But it's all true. "A great story, no?" she asks, smiling, as I struggle to get it all down in my notebook. "I know I'm the only nude dancer in Vegas who went to Woodstock and who also burned her draft card. And write this down, too. I'm also a socialist."

So into the night we go, Andrea telling me her life story, and in so doing revealing not only a dramatic personal journey but also some remarkable insight into how Las Vegas is the repository and incubator for tens of thousands of Americans who have been given—in defiance of Scotty Fitzgerald's nostrum—a unique environment in which to develop and live out their second acts.

What's perhaps most relevant is this: born into a well-educated and firmly middle-class Manhattan family "and summarily pronounced a male," George, as she was named, was troubled if not tortured with a gender identity crisis from early on. While her brother went off peacefully to marry legendary writer Jack Kerouac's daughter, Andrea struggled with drugs and alcohol and dropped out of art school. Taking on a tough macho posture, she married a stripper. "But it sort of fell apart," she now laughs, "when she caught me using her makeup."

After completing her gender transition, as she had said earlier, she returned to her job at Boeing and was "shoved upstairs with the secretaries." Fighting off a bout of depression, Andrea caught herself driving by a strip bar on her way home from the Boeing plant one night. "I don't know what it was," she says. "But I went and watched and said to myself, 'I'm in as good a shape as these girls. I can do that as well as they can, probably better.'" She auditioned for a job and got it. "It was definitely a second puberty for me, there was something really empowering about suddenly being a woman and doing the dancing."

After six months of moonlighting between the dance gig and Boeing and as a self-described "Excel buff," she says she started wondering how much she could make dancing full time. "Obviously, Las Vegas was the Mecca for me," she says. "I took a six week leave from Boeing and came to Vegas with eight hundred dollars in my account, not knowing a soul. I walked right into the Olympic Gardens Club and bullshitted them, pretending that I was a veteran at this, and told them I was available on Tuesday nights only. They told me it was the slow season and to come back in three months. What did I know? Next day I walked into the Déjà Vu and they hired me on the spot. Three or four weeks later I mailed in my resignation letter to Boeing. Hell, I was making $2,500 a week right off the bat. And I loved every minute of it—hanging out with men, each one telling me how beautiful I was. Within a year I bought a house for a quarter of a million dollars."

Andrea lost the house in the post-9/11, post-dotcom economic slump. "Ask any dancer what she invests in," she jokes, "and she'll give you the same answer. Boobs and real estate. It really hurt to give up that house. I still can't believe it."

Now she fears that, with the political heat coming down on the dance clubs, with the vice cops stepping up ticketing arrests inside the clubs since passage of the new regulation, and with her own elevated activist profile rankling the club owners, the future of her livelihood may be in dire peril. In a city of gambling, Andrea Hackett's staking it all on trying to build her still-struggling dancers' association into a powerful union that can level out the playing field for some of the most precarious workers in town. "All roads lead to one conclusion," she says. "Union." She's already made contact with a group of dancers looking to unionize in Texas. And eventually, she thinks, dancers are going to need a national organization. "I've already got the name figured. The United States Dancers Alliance. Or USDA," she says with a laugh, slapping her flank. "Get it?"

The campaign by casino interests to clamp down competition from the dance clubs plays out in other odd ways beyond the county lap-dance ordinance. For months now, the ACLU has been fighting blatantly discriminatory and laughably hypocritical advertising regulations at Vegas's McCarran International Airport—the eighth busiest in America. Wall-sized, illuminated ads for the big hotels, casinos, and their increasingly saucy shows inundate airport arrival lounges, ticketing areas, and even the cavernous baggage claim areas. Visitors can even check into some of the larger hotels in plush satellite offices near the luggage carousels. The airport is a public-owned facility but it has commissioned a private agency to manage the lucrative display advertising spaces and that company has enforced a rule banning any advertising in the airport from the dance clubs, saying it would offend their other clients. The company, Vidia, perhaps not coincidentally, is a subsidiary of gambling giant MGM Mirage.

"This is ridiculous. There is a clear economic motive here. The [casino corporations] don't want competitors advertising. But it's a public space that has to be open to everyone," says the Nevada ACLU's chief, Gary Peck, when I meet with him at his home near UNLV. One more middle-aged transplanted East-coaster in this city of domestic refugees, the fast-talking and infectiously gregarious Peck is often a lonely solider for civil liberties in a city supposedly founded on the principles of uninhibited personal freedom. "When it comes to freedom," Peck says, "Las Vegas is the best and the worst of places. A real paradox."

This morning, Peck and I are joined by a frequent and key partner in most of his skirmishes, attorney Allen Lichtenstein who serves as the ACLU's general counsel and who also represents several "adult industry" clients, including some of the smaller dance clubs. Together they have fought the local and state authorities on, among other issues, police harassment and racial profiling, and harsh treatment of the homeless, and working with support from the clergy and the unions (as well as Andrea Hackett) they recently won a partial victory in rolling back an onerous practice of forcing increasingly varied groups of workers to acquire and purchase work permit cards—a thinly veiled revenue shake-down racket run by the police. The ACLU also fights a perpetual defensive war for preservation of public space against the gaming corporations that have tried to privatize the sidewalks in front of their hotels, and which have mostly succeeded in enclosing and effectively privatizing several blocks of downtown's Fremont Street. But Peck argues that it is, rather predictably, on the core issue of sex, that Vegas is "absolutely schizophrenic."

"People are lured here by sex. Yet the local officials, I can tell you without any reservation, are absolutely obsessed with controlling sex," Peck says excitedly, raising his hands into the air, laughing and shrugging. "There's an economic motive, for sure. But it goes way beyond that into areas that border on the perverse."

"This is the ultimate company state," Lichtenstein says joining in. "The powers that be want to totally control the environment. It's Nevada's libertarian spirit versus the industry, and everything here is measured strictly on how it affects tourism. Everyone knows that that brothels are legal in several Nevada counties. Yet advertising for those brothels is illegal here in Las Vegas. Why? Simply because [the casinos] don't want you to leave here. You don't think that the powers that be actually mind prostitution, do you? It helps their business. They just don't want it visible from the street."

"In the meantime," Lichtenstein continues, "we have abysmal social services, abysmal mental health care, and aggressive police prone to rousting. The coroner's inquest process has never found a single Las Vegas police officer culpable of an unlawful civilian killing. This is a bad place to get shot or strangled by a cop. We have a split mentality. We are Sin City, supposedly. But also supposedly, an all-American city."

As to the new county lap-dance ordinance, Lichtenstein agrees with Andrea Hackett that it's motivated by money. But his theory is more complex than Andrea's. It might not be a battle only against the dance clubs, but perhaps, he says, also *among* them. Some of the club owners are politically well-connected and it's not always clear just who's muscling whom. "There's been a real proliferation of these clubs," he says. "What we are seeing now is a definite move by local government to thin out the competition at the behest of certain powerful operators. There's a crackdown, but without any outcry or demand from the public for a cleanup."

I leave Peck's house, heading toward the Strip and turning on the radio. As if on cue, on comes a lengthy news report about a dramatic, if not downright cinematic police raid overnight at one of the more notorious dance clubs. It seems like the old days in

Vegas all of a sudden. In a pre-dawn maneuver, a joint task force of as many as one hundred agents from the FBI, DEA, IRS, and local Metro police intelligence, two rifle-toting SWAT teams, some wearing ski masks and armed with federal search warrants, barged into the Crazy Horse Too club right down from the Déjà Vu, and spent long hours inside confiscating files, credit card records and processing machines, cash registers and every document they could glom onto. News reports later in the day said the warrants authorized the police to seize papers "which would demonstrate the existence of tribute payments made to La Cosa Nostra crime families for allowing businesses to operate in Las Vegas." The cops were also looking for records that might document "the identity of those persons who may have a hidden ownership in the club."

The Crazy Horse Too already had the worst of reputations among the dance clubs and had made plenty of news before; mostly hair-raising accounts of customers getting ripped off inside and then beaten silly by the goonish bouncers. A federal investigation into the operation preceded today's raid by fifteen months. The registered owner of the club, Rick Rizzolo—in California when the raid was conducted—has been linked by his critics to mobsters Joey Cusamano, Fred Pascente, and Chris Petti. All three are listed in Nevada's so-called Black Book which bars them from entering any casino and the Feds suspect that Rizzolo's ownership of the club might be merely a front for mobbed-up pals who could be secret partners. One key employee of Rizzolo's club, Vinny Faraci, is the son of Bonanno crime family operative "Johnny Green" Faraci. Another coworker is a prime suspect in an incident that occurred two years ago when a hapless tourist wound up with a broken neck after an argument in front of the club door over his modest bar bill.

But Rick Rizzolo also has another class of friends—many of Nevada's ranking politicians. A year ago, in the spring of 2002, the dean of Vegas political writers, John L. Smith, penned an acerbic column recounting his own recent dinner at Piero's, a swanky Vegas restaurant whose owner is also a close friend of Rizzolo's. It's not that Smith was shocked to see Nevada's Republican governor, Kenny Guinn, and his wife Dema come over warmly to greet Rizzolo, who was holding court with a table full of friends. It's just that there was also a California undercover detective watching the spectacle from a nearby chair. "[The detective] smiled at the scene," Smith wrote. "In his home state, such a meeting between governor and topless entrepreneur might be front-page news. In Nevada, it's merely one example of Rizzolo's amazing circle of contacts, which stretch from the governor's mansion to the fringes of the Chicago mob."

Rizzolo's political immunity stems from a simple equation, as Smith pointed out. His political contributions average as high one hundred thousand dollars a year, sometimes larger than that of casino companies, and have been generously spread among candidates for judgeships, county commissioners, city councilmen, several Democratic legislative and congressional races, the Democratic National Committee, the Nevada Democratic Party, and the 2000 Republican presidential campaign of George W. Bush. In 2001 Rizzolo shook out forty thousand dollars in donations for Vegas Mayor Oscar Goodman, a former mob lawyer who has represented not only Cusamano and Rizzolo but also some world-class gangsters including Meyer Lansky and Tony Spilotro.

Rizzolo's biggest political buddy, however, has been Republican city councilman Mike McDonald, a former Vegas cop no less, who was investigated a few years ago about his relationship with the club owner, but was never charged with any crime. Back in 1999 Rizzolo was able to expand his club without having to fuss with the usual permits and inspections after the councilman helped clear the path by getting rid of a porno bookstore next door. McDonald, who says he never took a campaign contribution from Rizzolo because it wouldn't look right, doesn't hide his friendship with Rizzolo, and he told the press that just two nights before the federal raid on the Crazy Horse Too he had dropped Rizzolo off at the club after a fund-raiser for a local candidate for judge. Most confounding, the city granted favors to the club at the same time that Metro police logged hundreds of incident calls at the venue. But at no point did the city or its agencies challenge Rizzolo's licensing and permits.

The last significant political scandal that shook Vegas was nearly two decades ago when the FBI's undercover Operation Yobo pried back the lid on local corruption and tagged five big-gun pols with felony convictions. Former state senator Floyd Lamb served nine months in prison for taking twenty-three thousand dollars in bribes from undercover agents, former Clark County commissioner Jack Petitti got a six month term for taking five thousand dollars, and Harry Claiborne became the first federal judge in a half-century to be impeached and removed from office. Current Mayor Goodman was a former partner of Claiborne's and represented him during his two criminal trials and his congressional impeachment.

Opening the pages of the local *Review-Journal* and *Sun* to sample the ample coverage of the raid this week on the Crazy Horse Too and of its fallout, I'm hit with the unmistakable stench of a much bigger political scandal, involving sex, "made" guys and back-room pay-offs just straining to burst wide open. *Las Vegas Sun* columnist Jon Ralston wonders aloud if the bill that the political establishment has racked up by its shameless dancing over the years for Rizzolo is finally coming due or if this new scandal will simply gust and then subside like one more desert sirocco. And, moreover, who's to say that the alleged influence-buying of Rizzolo is much different than the business-as-usual side of Nevada's corporate politics—like when the Mandalay Resort Group, in one twenty-four-hour period, laid three hundred grand in legal contributions on Kenny Guinn to as much as lock down his gubernatorial candidacy.

In the meantime, the ghosts of Bugsy Siegel and Ice Pick Willy must be having some hearty laughs watching their own version of *Poltergeist,* as the old-time muck of Sin City bubbles up and threatens to tarnish the gleaming corporate exterior of the New Vegas. Ralston writes: "Nothing so captures the conjunction of Old Las Vegas with the new, of the schizophrenic clash of a sinful background and sanitized façade than does the now stripped bare investigation of Rick Rizzolo."

Doubling Down

I T's COMING UP ON three in the morning in the dark heart of the Mandalay Bay Casino and every Blackjack hand landing in front of me is stiff as a board. Every fourteen-, fifteen- and sixteen-count in the entire casino, it seems, is gravitating toward me. And every hit I take pulls out a hand-busting high card. Ziggy, the chatty dealer, meanwhile, nonchalantly flips over one pair of face cards after another, ruthlessly cutting down my pile of green-and-red twenty-five dollar "quarter" chips—or "checks," as they're called on the casino floor.

Sure, as in every casino on the Strip, everything is designed to imprison me here: its labyrinth no-exit layout; the absence of any clocks, phones, or windows; the cashier cage, which is inconspicuously hidden in the back; the ubiquitous ATMs that dispense nothing smaller than C-note denominations; an endless flow of free drinks (I'm on my fourth Wild Turkey); the loud clanging of coins in acoustically-hyped metal trays; the disorienting flashing and flickering lights of the slots and video machines; the brightly colored chips themselves—like play money, so much less painful to push forward than the twenty-five or one hundred dollars in cash each one costs. The room temperature perfectly calibrated to a womb-like comfort level. The air exchange cycle so accelerated that there's enough fresh gushing oxygen in this hangar-sized room to burnish the cheeks of an entire army of zombies to a rosy, baby-pink.

Truth is, however, I'm here completely voluntarily—at least technically—as I'm in the worst position a player can find himself: what's known as "chasin' the money." Nervously, and somewhat recklessly, getting deeper and deeper into the game, spending more and more, trying not so much to get ahead but to at least win back some if not all of what's already been lost.

I'm not sure quite how I got in this fix—though I've been here enough times before. But here I was alone at the table, yakking it up with Ziggy, as I often do, savoring the tales of his late gambler father who ran the Desert Inn's original bar, and what was a relaxed, no-stress, give-and-take round of near-even play somehow took an ugly and rather precipitous dip.

That's being polite. More accurately, I'm in a sort of freefall. Blackjack is a game that can simmer literally for hours at a break-even pace. Mathematically, of every one hundred hands, the dealer should win forty-eight, you should win forty-four, and you should tie eight times. That's, of course, the theoretical odds and it's sometimes more or less the concrete case. But, without warning, the game might start to swing way up or way down, much like the needle of a Cal Tech seismograph in the midst of a 7.0 earthquake.

And right now the ground underneath me is rocking and

rolling and I am way down. Down, all of sudden, in just the last ten minutes or so. In much deeper than I want to be for what was intended as just as friendly play with one of my favorite Vegas dealers. I bought five hundred dollars in chips an hour ago, and now my last surviving two tokens—fifty dollars in total—are sitting on the betting line.

Ziggy pitches me an eleven, a seven-four combination. The one card he's showing is a red jack—a ten. Apart from an ace, it's the best card a dealer can have as his up card. If his hole card, the card he has face down on the table, is a seven, eight, nine, ten, jack, queen, or king he'll have a made hand and he won't bust out. His ten-up means I have no choice to keep hitting, to get at least seventeen, hopefully higher, without going over 21. Ziggy's red jack is a formidable, intimidating up-card.

But my eleven is marginally better. Almost a third of the cards in the deck, theoretically, have a value of ten—meaning I've got at least an almost one-in-three shot that when I hit, when I draw a card, I'll end up with an unbeatable hand of twenty-one.

This is the moment to double down, to double my bet and take one card only. But the risk is high and so is the bet. Is this really how I want to spend a hundred bucks? This slight advantage is only one more mathematical construct and not even remotely a certainty. My mind begins to race. My last two checks are in play on the betting line—so to double down I'll have to break another hundred-dollar bill thanks to those doctored ATMs. Half of the hundred will go right on the betting line to double the bet. If I lose, I know for certain I'll play the other two chips left over and then I could be in for six hundred dollars. Yet, if I don't double and I win, I'll regret my cowardice for hours to come. And what if I don't double and I still lose? Will I walk away, admit and accept defeat, and go to bed? Or will I buy in for more chips anyway, hoping that my losing cycle is about to turn upward?

A recent poll by Nevada's largest marketing research group shows that only 17 percent of people coming to Vegas say they plan to gamble. That compares with 38 percent who say they are coming primarily for "sightseeing." But what sights? Evidently, the casinos. The same poll says this same average tourist will visit eight casinos while here. And in the end, say Vegas tourist authorities, regardless of what they tell their spouses, children, office mates, or marketing pollsters for that matter, a whopping 87 percent of all tourists will spend an average of four hours a day gambling. I'm one of them. Though tonight, I wish I weren't. Or do I?

The decision I now have to make is the juice of gambling. It's the buzz. And this one's a no-brainer. The double-down bet is the smart bet, the right bet, the strategic bet. Out of my pocket comes another Ben Frank. Ziggy flattens it out on the table for the benefit of the all-seeing Eye-in-the-Sky cameras. Then he holds it up briefly to the light and runs his fingers expertly over the bill's texture. "Change—one hundred," he calls out to the pit boss leaning on his podium, a pudgy, balding, middle-aged man with drooping eyelids who, no doubt, is wishing everyone here, including me, would lose as quickly as possible and let him go home maybe a half-hour early.

With his left hand, Ziggy stuffs the hundred dollar bill into the slotted mouth of the table and shoves it all the way down with his plastic plunger. With his right, he scoops four $25 chips from his tray, loudly clacks two of them down next to my upturned seven-four, doubling my bet, and seamlessly slides the remaining two chips toward me. Ziggy straightens his back, which is always tormenting him, wishes me good luck, and with sharp-angled military precision pulls a single card from the dealer's shoe and, as ceremony has it, snaps it face down and perfectly perpendicular to my other two cards. In an effortlessly swift move he mastered long ago over his twenty-seven years of dealing experience, he uses his upturned card, the red jack, to seamlessly flip over his down card. Another red jack who seems to be smirking. Shit. Ziggy's got a pair of jakes, a daunting twenty.

My stomach knots as he reaches to turn over the one card I've bought for an additional fifty bucks. In this game players can't touch the cards. They can only shovel money onto the table. If my double-down card that Ziggy turns over is a nine, we push, tying each other with a twenty. Any other card, except a face card or a ten, and I'll be down yet another hundred in the middle of the night.

The card Ziggy flips for me is a hefty black ten, a hand-winning twenty-one in total. I've survived another hand. Ziggy pays me off with a single, black one-hundred-dollar chip, an unspoken invitation to play it. I accept, pulling back my four quarter checks and leaving the black one-hundred on the betting line. Ziggy deals me out two eights—a sixteen. He's showing a six up. It's the dealer's worst card, one he breaks on more than half the time.

My only option is to split the eights into two hands, at twice the price. You always split eights, even against a dealer's ace. But with a dealer showing a stiff six, double eights can be a real money-maker. I split the twin-eights into two hands, tossing down the additional four quarter chips I just pulled back next to one of the eights. Now I've got two hundred dollars in play, but I'm in excellent position. Excellent if I win. Meanwhile, this friendly twenty-five-dollar-a-hand game has escalated into a two-hundred-dollar-a-shot stomach twister.

Ziggy slaps another card face up on my first eight. A three, totaling eleven, and he smiles knowing that only a fool wouldn't double down again. I cash another hundred and this time the whole amount reinforces the bet on that single hand—two hundred dollars. I ask Ziggy to toss me the one extra card, face up. I get a six, giving me a seventeen. "It's what we call a mother-in-law," quips Ziggy. "You'd like to get rid of it, but you can't." Now I'm in for seven hundred dollars.

Seventeen on the first hand is not very reassuring. I've got to play the other hand and hope for something better. Call it the best or the worst of luck, but Ziggy fishes me out yet another eight. He doesn't even wait for my nod as he moves the new card to the side of its twin, knowing full well I'm going to split *those* eights as well for yet another hundred bucks

The card Ziggy throws on top my second eight is a two. We both break out laughing. Scratch that idea about a 7.0 earthquake. This a nine plus on the Richter scale. With the cards breaking this way, we both know that I'm trapped in the middle of a tsunami-sized wave of luck—we just don't know if I'm surfing the crest of it or if I'm about to get sucked away in its merciless tube. My ten against his six is another double down. When I buy that black chip to match what's already there, I'm in for nine hundred dollars this evening. The bet made, my next card is a five! A fucking fifteen, a hand that beats nothing. It makes my mother-in-law seventeen hand look like Cameron Diaz.

I've got one more eight to play and it better be good. I get an ace of spades from Ziggy. An ace counts eleven or one, so I've got a nine or what's called a soft nineteen—a high hand. But Ziggy hesitates before turning over his hole card and playing his hand. He lightly and expectantly raps the back of his knuckles on the table next to my hand, his palm half-open. He knows what's coming. It's a move he's taught me some months before in some other late-night session.

What the fuck, I figure. In for nine hundred, in for a grand, what's the difference? Another hundred dollars in. A high-wire double-down on a soft nineteen, counting it as nine, betting I'll draw a ten bringing me back to a strong nineteen and that Ziggy'll bust out with his stiff six up. But making this bet means tossing out a relatively good nineteen.

Ziggy throws me my last card, a king. So now with a thousand dollars invested in the game, with six hundred on the line and a measly fifty dollars in reserve, at least I've got one decent hand—the nineteen. And two weak ones.

Ziggy flips over his hole card and instead of the ten I wanted to see, the ten that would give him a sixteen and push him to the edge of busting, he instead shows a five. Five-six, a deadly eleven. Deadly for me. I can as much as hear the fifty-foot wave above my head about to pound me into the rocks. Everything in me says I'm about to walk away a thousand dollars poorer. Sitting with eleven, Ziggy's due to pull a face card next and wipe out all three of my two-hundred-dollar hands with a twenty-one. He pauses and gives me a sympatheic glance, as he also knows what's coming. Not only is Ziggy a friend, but like most dealers he's pained by my coming loss. Losing players rarely toke, or tip, a dealer.

But when Ziggy plucks his next card out of the shoe, he pulls out an ace of spades, giving him twelve. Two seconds of reprieve before he hits again and banks my chips. But then out comes the queen I expected on the previous card. Ziggy busts out, breaking with a twenty-two. He neatly stacks up two black hundred-dollar chips in front of each of my three hands. Between my bet, my winnings and my two quarter chips in reserve, I've got $1,250 on the table. I've gone from losing $450 to winning $250 in about 90 seconds with a thousand-dollar risk in between. The tide's definitely running my way. The tightness in my chest has subsided, the flutter in my stomach is more anticipation than dread. I should go to bed and walk away a winner. I keep on playing.

"Blackjack validates you as a human being. You feel great when you win because you made enough good decisions to justify your playing the game," says fifty-five-year old Max Rubin, a guy you might call the Apostle of Blackjack. "Blackjack is not only the most beatable game in Vegas, but it's the one that requires the most skill, that depends most on the moves you make, the decisions you make. Play Blackjack and you're much more in control."

Moving out to Vegas from Texas in the '60s on a college scholarship, Rubin says he stayed in school to "beat the draft." At age twenty-one he got a dealer's job at Binion's Horseshoe casino, and has worked a jumble of gambling jobs since, including pit boss and casino manager until he quit ten years ago. He's made a bundle with his best-selling book, *Comp City,* a guide to squeezing freebies out of the casinos, and currently works as a gambling consultant on both sides of the gaming table.

His real passion, though, is Blackjack. And every January he hosts the annual Blackjack Ball in the casino-like basement of his spacious home, a fête that attracts some of the top players in the world, including members of the infamous, full-time professional "teams" that systematically move like locusts through the casinos, silently but methodically grazing away at gaming profits. "There are action gamblers and escape gamblers," he says. "The action players go for Blackjack or craps. The escape players are on the machines. But think of how each game makes you feel. Ever meet a machine player who thinks he's James Bond? I don't think so."

"Say you've got fifty thousand dollars," Rubin says over cold drinks in his living room. "And you open up a little chicken stand or something. What do you think your chances are of making it? Not great. Compare that to Blackjack. You've got a *much* better chance there to make fifty grand. Sure, you're still the underdog, but aren't we always the underdogs in life? At least in Blackjack, you're playing at near-even odds. Where else does that happen in life?"

I'll leave that last question for the philosophers. But Rubin's right about Blackjack's odds—there's simply no better game to play unless you own the casino. Play the right version of the game and have at least a basic understanding of what you're doing, and the house advantage can be less than one-half a percent. A lot less.

Compare that with out-and-out sucker games, "house games," like the Wheel of Fortune which mills out as much as a 24 percent edge for the house; or the bingo-like Keno which can tilt at a 33 percent disadvantage to the player. Roulette—over which you have no control and which requires no skills other than the physical ability to keep plunking down chips—leaves more than a 5 percent advantage to the house (how could it not when it pays thirty-five-to-one even though there are thirty-eight numbers on the wheel?). Slot machines—devices I have vowed to never stoop to play—can legally retain as much as 25 percent of what's fed through them. Even machines that "guarantee" a 98 percent or 99 percent return do so *over the long run,* the long run being a million pulls or so of the handle—which means you might catch a very unlucky half-million spins in which you *lose* 98 or 99 percent or 200 or 300 percent or more of your money.

Video poker, the crack cocaine of modern gambling, can offer attractive odds like Blackjack's, but that's if you play "computer perfect." But sitting alone for hours in front of a video screen and pushing buttons every eight seconds hardly sounds like fun. Craps is also a close game, one I will occasionally play for fun and because the old-school croupiers so colorfully narrate the game. But I refuse to submit my fortune to the literal roll of the dice and will not invest any substantial sum in them. Mind-numbingly simple baccarat is for very stupid and very rich people—so no thanks. Live Texas Hold-em can pay off in the millions, if you make it into the World Series of Poker. But that's a game that demands too much skill. In poker, you're not playing your cards. You're playing the other players. No thanks.

So-called "carnival games" like Caribbean Stud Poker, Three-Card Poker, and Casino War are exactly that, stacked, one-sided, carnie rip-off games for the terminally naïve. They should be played only as a last-gasp alternative to Russian roulette, whose odds are only slightly worse.

That leaves Blackjack. But you've got to play it right and bet it right. Just about every casino gift shop sells little laminated strategy cards which tell you when to hit and when to stay. They're valuable cheat sheets and sold by the casinos for a buck or two only because so few people bother to pay them any attention. They ought to. In very abbreviated shorthand, and with lots of exceptions to the rule and a dozen or so nuances, if you can bust and the dealer can bust with one card, you stay and let him play.

Likewise, if the dealer's showing an up card which would give him a "made" hand of seventeen or more with a ten in the hole, then hit right through a sixteen.

Easy enough. But experts say as many as one in six hands of

Vegas Blackjack are played wrong. My personal observation is that it's more like twice that number. That explains why a game that gives the house an average 1 to 2 percent edge nevertheless generates a per table 11 to 15 percent profit. In spite of a proliferation of specialized how-to-books, web sites and seminars, "the average players are about as bad as they've always been," says Rubin. "They don't really know how to play, they don't want to know, and don't want to learn. A lot of people think they're playing basic strategy. But only about 10 percent really do."

There's a bravado aspect to action gambling and men, especially young men, are reticent to admit that there might actually be some studying to be done before throwing money on the table and are instead deluded into believing that with enough testosterone and tequila they can bulldoze their way to winning. How flummoxed they get when some chubby grandma of a dealer, who can't wait to get back home and finish her quilting project, comes in and annihilates them in ten minutes.

There's also a number of common Blackjack hands that require strategic moves that are counter-intuitive, that to the average player *feel* wrong, that seemingly contradict common sense. No matter. Eights should be split against a dealer's ten or even his nine. Just as you should hit sixteen against any dealer's card of seven or higher, or doubling a ten against a dealer's ten or an eleven against his face card. And so on.

Tons of players brush aside the coldly logical side of the game and prefer their own "systems." But that's how the mega-resorts got built. My own mother, a fanatical Blackjack player, taught me to play at an early age—and she taught me completely wrong, warning me to never hit a twelve or higher under any circumstances. It took my first decade as an adult to unlearn her system which did little but make her a perennial loser.

One corner of Vegas I know she didn't visit is the harshly lit, hard-floored Gamblers Book Club on the nondescript downtown corner of Eleventh and Charleston. Opened in 1969 by casino floorman John Luckman (I kid you not) and his wife Edna, the store today books a million dollars a year's worth of sales. Its Blackjack section alone stocks more than a hundred titles. "It's a new generation we got out there. I can't tell you how hot our gambling software is nowadays," says its new owner, sixty-three-year-old Howard Schwartz. An owlish, wise-cracking intellectual, with not a faint resemblance to Woody Allen, Schwartz, who lists being a Nader Raider on a long list of former occupations, was hired as store manager over the phone twenty-five years ago after "burning out" as a school teacher in Littleton, Colorado. He inherited the store outright a few months ago when Edna Luckman passed on.

"When I first got here," he says, "I was afraid to answer the phone about gambling questions. I didn't know anything about it." That was then. Nowadays, Schwartz's betting opinions are eagerly sought out. Indeeed, our conversation is interrupted by a call from *Horse Player* magazine, asking him to write one of the many articles and reviews he publishes every year. And it's not just magazines and newspapers who call on Howard.

"I get calls all the time directly from the tables," he says. "From the casino floor, even directly from cell phones at poker tables in the Taj Mahal in Atlantic City. 'What do I do with this hand I'm holding?' is the most common question I get. My answer is usually: 'Pray!' " A good friend of Archie Karras who's known for losing eighteen million dollars in poker and craps, Howard says he has little taste himself for gambling. "In twenty-four years here I'm ahead seventeen hundred dollars—about eighty-two cents a week," he says. Nor is Schwartz much of a fan of the New Vegas, decrying the "sterile corporate atmosphere, the paranoiac, over-efficient way of going about things."

Undoubtedly, Schwartz's own bookstore has made its own contribution to the casino clampdown on Blackjack. The scores of how-to-win books the store offers all convey the same basic advice in some form or another: it's about counting the cards, stupid. At least know if there's a lot of high cards or low cards left in the deck. The more high cards, the greater the chance the dealer will bust and the bigger your bets should be.

Until the now legendary Ed Thorpe published his classic *Beat The Dealer* in 1962, Vegas casino Blackjack was a simple matter of one hand-dealt deck of fifty-two cards. Thorpe's book touched off a still ongoing battle of strategic measures and counter-measures. To thwart freshly-educated card counters anxious to try out Thorpe's system, Vegas casinos started shaving their own games. They added a second deck of cards, doubling the difficulty of counting the cards. Then as many as six or eight decks became more and more common. To reduce cheating by dealers and to house such a bulging mass of cards, the box-like shoe replaced the cradled hands of the dealer. Hand-dealt single-deck, and even double-deck Blackjack became an endangered species, relegated increasingly to the less glitzy off-Strip, low-end, and downtown casinos.

"It's a simple formula," says Max Rubin. "The fewer decks, the better for the player." The advantage of single deck is the so-called Effect of Removal. "Pick up a five-six combination, an eleven for example, and when you double down looking for a high card, you already know that at least one-fourth of the fives and sixes are already gone from the deck," he says. In a six-deck game, by contrast, there could still be dozens of those hand-spoiling cards still lurking in the dealer's shoe.

But as the casinos turned more and more to multi-decks,

computer-armed player strategists came up with and published new and efficient ways to count or at least keep track of what was left in the Blackjack shoe.

The casinos are only happy to escalate the psychological war. About a decade ago, automatic shuffle machines started showing up, putting an end to another player advantage—advanced shuffle tracking. The machines also sped up the game by about 20 percent, meaning inevitably accelerated players' losses. Then over the last few years the bigger casinos took it up another notch and started deploying *perpetual* shuffle machines. After each hand the cards are fed back into the whirring black box, creating an endless game with no breaks and no potential whatsoever for counting anything, except your losses.

The newest generation of casinos, like the Palms, aimed at the youngest generation of players bereft of any historic memory of the way Blackjack ought to be played, further shave the game by loading down their Blackjack tables with myriad and steeply disadvantageous "fun" side bets. Put an extra dollar—or if you're dumb enough—ten dollars on each hand in the Lucky Ladies version of Blackjack and reap a big payoff if the two cards you're tossed are matching queens. The only lucky ladies in this game are the nice gals in the hard-count room, merrily toting up the increased Blackjack drop.

Hawkeyed floor supervisors, backed up by experts peering at the camera monitors, scan the players' moves, relentlessly searching for signs of card-counting. It's not illegal. It's just not tolerated. When a pit boss spies some schmo who regularly bets ten dollar a hand suddenly upping his wager to one hundred dollar or more, he figures the guy has been counting and knows what's coming. With increasing frequency, the floormen enforce a maximum four-to-one spread, not allowing any player to ever bet four times more than his or her basic minimum. Try to bet more and you won't get your hands smashed or your knees broken, you'll just be asked to leave.

The Hilton has perhaps gone the farthest in striking back at skillful Blackjack players. At the cost of about twenty thousand dollars each, small, rather inconspicuous "Mindplay" infrared scanners installed on several of its twenty-one tables build up-to-the instant computerized databases of how each hand has been played by each player—a literal gold mine of research in devising new house advantages and in revealing and disarming evolving player strategies.

Most casinos offer some slightly varied menu of Blackjack games. But overall, the shuffle machines and stacked "fun" mutations are rapidly taking over the floor, while relatively pure games of single deck are still found in just a few downtown casinos. Most players, by my observation, don't even notice these details, never stopping to think for a moment what difference a half-dozen additional decks or a perpetual "Quick Draw" shuffle machine might or might not make in their game. "I've had at least ten people sit down at my Quick Draw table with a hundred dollar bill in their hand, wanting to buy chips and waiting and waiting and waiting for the game to end," Ziggy once told me. "And they can't figure out why the end never comes, why I never have to shuffle or even take a break. Experienced players hate the machine and never come back."

The majority of players, at least the recreational players, are not very experienced, however, and they figure they're going to lose anyway. And they're right. "Most play to have fun and that's OK," says Rubin. "In any case, playing strategies work over the long run. In the short run, it's all about luck. Luck overcomes all."

Back to that late night game with Ziggy at the Mandalay Bay. I, in fact, do prefer single-deck games—games that this slick Strip casino is too smart to play. But, as Rubin says, I also want to have a good time playing. Playing Blackjack isn't at all just about the money. I'm not sure, in my case at least, that it has anything to do with the money. There are the great stories that percolate around the table and that can keep me anchored there for hours. Ziggy relishes recounting the tale of the little old lady who last year walked into the Mandalay and won a mind-scrambling twenty-eight hands in a row, a historic, once-in-a-lifetime run that would net trash bags full of cash for even the most modest gambler. Yet, this woman, stubbornly refusing to ever raise her bet beyond the $5 minimum, or to ever let any portion of winnings ride, walked away with only $140 to show for what must have been a record streak. Then there's the opposite tale Ziggy tells: the guy who walked into Binion's Horseshoe and started with a thousand-dollar buy-in. A few hours later he had run his table holdings to a stratospheric $460,000. Instead of walking away rich, he kept playing for hours more and quit when he was down to only nine thousand dollars. The next night he comes back to chase the chimerical winnings of the day before. Soon, he loses all nine thousand dollars—plus an extra grand.

Ziggy's warmth and wit, his ongoing sly narration about everything happening around us in the casino, his retelling of Vegas lore, make it worth it to me to now and then tough out the turbulent swings of a multi-deck Blackjack game. So after I win that triple hand of split-up eights, I stay on at the table, even as Ziggy goes off shift and is replaced by a young Asian woman I've never seen before who, unsmilingly and silently, whips the cards onto the table at a blurring, lightning pace, as fast as maybe 100 hands an hour.

I make no attempt to count the cascade of cards rushing out of the dealer's shoe, she's just too fast for my sort of rudimentary card tracking. But I, nevertheless, play every hand meticulously, never straying from basic strategy, never playing hunches, guesses, or feelings. It's a good run. My double-downs are making it, the dealer's busting regularly, and I'm getting a generous helping of winning nineteens and twenties. Three hours later, I rise from the table, drained and exhausted.

As I drive up the Strip through a gray desert dawn, the casino road-signs still blaring at full voltage, my strained eyes dry and aching, my throat parched from the casino smoke, my empty stomach grumbling, my back smarting, my legs numb, my ears clogged from the incessant clanging of the casino, my brain barely flickering under a thick coat of fuzz. I have no idea how I will make it through the interviews I've booked for this afternoon.

But I'm happy. I think of the $1,475 in winnings I've just taken from the Mandalay and I feel like a genius. Though, in my gut, I know Max Rubin is right. It was mostly pure dumb luck.

Ziggy's Story

HAVING LUNCH WITH ZIGGY a few days later, seeing him in his civvies, in ironed jeans and a soft, knit, white sweater, his grayish hair in a neat pompadour, instead of finding him in his standard dealer uniform of black pants, white shirt, and the Mandalay's tight goldish-green vest, reminds me a bit of the first time I saw one of my junior high school teachers moonlighting one summer at Sears, wearing a brightly colored short sleeve shirt instead of his usual tie and jacket. Sometimes your notion or image of others is indelibly, and unfairly, wrapped up with their day job.

Ziggy's been dealing Blackjack for nearly three decades, but that's, indeed, just something he does for a living—in this case over a graveyard shift. But he just as well might be a high school teacher or an even an actuary. In every way he is a quiet, mannered, married, middle-class, middle American father of three girls in his late fifties who "hates card games," and never, ever gambles. "My grandmother made me play canasta with her all the time and I had to hold all fifteen cards in my hand," he says. "And on top of that, she cheated me." Eschewing the tables where he works and the slot machines that infest every corner of Vegas, right down to supermarkets and gas stations, Ziggy gets his real kicks watching TV with his wife or growing chili peppers in the garden of his comfortable, suburban home.

Yet Ziggy's personal rise to respectability and mainstream American living—via the gambling industry—almost perfectly mirrors and matches the evolution and transformation of Vegas itself. Call him a vivisection of Vegas.

His father, born in Sweden, jumped his merchant-marine ship at age twenty-four and disembarked in Los Angeles just in time to pick up some work during the 1932 Olympics. After he crashed into the car of Freeman Godfrey and took the injured actor to the hospital for treatment, he was adopted by a fast-lane Hollywood crowd. He worked on the production of *The Invaders* with Errol Flynn and even had a date with Gloria Swanson.

By the mid-'30s, Ziggy's father found himself tending bar at a mob-operated illegal casino at the Racquet Club in the Southern California desert resort of Palm Springs. Like so many other L.A.-area gamblers and what are daintily called their "associates," he "immigrated" to Vegas in 1939 and worked with the crew that established, two years later, the first Strip resort, the El Rancho Vegas. Next, he was taken on to design and run the bar at the Desert Inn when it opened in 1950, and from which he retired in the late '60s after Howard Hughes bought out the Dalitz gang.

Ziggy, meanwhile, says there was "nothing exceptional" about growing up as a child in the '40s and '50s in Las Vegas. Having classmates whose mothers were showgirls or whose fathers worked as dealers (one friend's father owned the Dunes) seemed perfectly natural. As a teenager, Ziggy yearned to be an electrician but couldn't break into a union that he says was rife with nepotism.

Gambling was all around him and it directly or indirectly provided most of the jobs. His first high school job was as a busboy at the Flamingo casino. "It wasn't long before I found the secret tunnels that Bugsy had built, including the one that ran to his private office," he says. "The mob guys weren't nearly as cool as they come off in the movies. A lot of them had no class at all. I remember seeing Sam Giancana at the Flamingo walking around, giving everyone, including me, a look-over. When the Mafia guys sold the Flamingo to Kerkorian I helped them steal the hotel's silver flatware," he remembers with a chuckle. "As a busboy they had me help load up all the silver into vans waiting in the back before they turned over the keys."

"One thing for sure during those days. There wasn't a lot of sleaze, not like today when people go to shows and don't bother to change out of their wife-beater T-shirts. Not in those days. The mob kept this city clean. You were a wife beater, or a child molester? Too bad. You'd simply get killed," he says.

Ziggy also remembers standing at the D.I. with his father watching Sammy Davis Jr. film the noted garbage truck scene where he sings the title song of the Rat Pack cult film, *Ocean's Eleven*. "I remember the Mafia guys as sort of tacky. But when it came to cool, nobody was as cool as Cesar Romero was in that film," he says. "Cesar Romero wasn't even that cool."

And while proclaiming no nostalgia whatsoever for the old times, there's no question that the then-waning era of mob-dominated Vegas was very, very good to Ziggy and allowed him to carve out a stable, respected, and lucrative profession. Dealers throughout Vegas are paid but minimum wage. The rest of their earnings derive from "tokes," the tips left by grateful or super-stitious players (the legions who are convinced that if they grease the dealer, he or she will emit subtle giveaways about his or her hole cards). In most casinos, the tokes are evenly split among the dealers on a nightly basis. And a recent *Dealers News* newsletter reports that while the nightly take totaled only about $60 in some of the off-Strip grind casinos, dealers at the upscale Bellagio and Mandalay were bagging as much as $225 in tips per shift—almost as much as the hundred-grand-a-year cocktail waitresses.

But you don't get a post at a place like the Mandalay without paying some dues. So the case with Ziggy, whose original break-in job as dealer at age twenty-one was at the Carousel—a down-town grinder which sported twenty-five-cent Blackjack and nickel craps. From there he followed a well-worn route up the casino ladder to the Slots-A-Fun, to the now closed and mob-riddled Thunderbird, finally hitting the big time when he was taken on at the Desert Inn in the early '80s.

"The D.I. was wonderful," Ziggy says. "The last place where they really treated the dealers as someone special. They gave us a lounge, fed us off the same restaurant menu, treated us above and beyond. George Deverall, who ran the place, brought in each dealer one by one and knew us each personally." When Deverall left, Ziggy followed him first to the Dunes, then to the Tropicana, and eventually to the Mandalay Bay.

"Dealing has always made me a comfortable living—even when I only brought home seventy-five cents that first day at the Carousel," Ziggy continues. "And I've always taken it seriously as a profession, as a career, as many in my generation have. Nowadays, a lot of the younger guys, the younger dealers, are transients. They come and go and see dealing more as a means to getting into something else, usually real estate."

"But not me. After twenty-seven years, every night when I walk up to the table I'm happy. When I have to leave, it's like, ugh. There's nothing else I'd rather be doing. I have fun with the game and fun with the people. I talk a lot and the bosses let me get away with it. I enjoy teaching the game, I want to help people play right. The more they win, the more they tip. I just love the people who come to my table. The best are the under-takers. They're really wild. This is the only place where they can come and party."

"What can I tell you? I just love my job. Haven't even taken a vacation in four years. I'd like to do this job forever."

When I ask Ziggy what's the worst part of his work, he hesi-tates and then laughs. "I can't think of anything, really," he protests. "Nothing. I rarely get an abusive player and when I do I usually get sympathy from the others at the table. Sometimes, I guess, it's hard to see nice people lose. I'd say 50 percent of the people who sit down really don't have a clue how to play. And something like 75 percent, maybe 85 percent of the players never make it away from the table with any of their money left. The hardest part of gambling, always, is walking away with your money."

On that last line, Ziggy has looked me squarely in the eyes. After having played at his table for hours and hours—days and days all told—over the last several months, I catch myself blushing at his observation. It's like he's my family doctor—someone who knows all the uncomfortable secrets.

Over coffee one afternoon, Bill Friedman—who once ran the Castaways and Silver Slipper casinos for Howard Hughes and who has recently completed an exhaustive book on effective casino design, tells me that becoming a Vegas dealer was his childhood aspiration. "At age seven my parents took me to Lake Tahoe and I spent all day watching the tables," he says. "When every other kid wanted to be a fireman, I wanted to be a dealer."

Fulfilling his dream, he left hometown Oakland and hit Las Vegas for his twenty-first birthday in 1964 and was soon hired on as a one-dollar-an-hour shill for the downtown Fremont Hotel. A shill was a casino employee who'd pose as a player, encouraging others to join in the action. "Back then the Fremont was a great high-roller dice place," he says. "They'd put forty of us shills on the swing shift because they wanted at least six players at each crap table. I'd come to work with my black'n'whites in a bag hoping some dealer would get sick and I'd get a chance to sub and show my stuff as a dealer."

It's doubtful that many of the new generation of Vegas dealers have the background of a Ziggy or a Bill Friedman, with the game literally in their blood. Most of them now come to their jobs after a stint in one of the dealer's schools, institutions with all the romance of a real-estate-license-exam academy. A number of these training grounds come and go in Vegas, but about a half-dozen of them are stable, entrenched schools that together crank out thousands of new dealers per year.

Former Nebraska farm boy, and former dealer, Nick Kallos has run his Casino Gaming School, located on the second floor of an unassuming commercial mall just east of the Strip, for the last fourteen years. On a weekday morning, about two dozen of his students, literally of all ages, shapes, and races, are studiously practicing their craft. The newest students repetitively pitch cards onto a tabletop shelf and watch their own movements in the mirror. Others practice shuffling, "stitching and lacing" the decks in a pile, chip counting, stripping and stacking, "protecting the deck" when it's hand-held, and properly peeking at hole cards without revealing them to the players. At a corner table, a master dealer teaches management of live poker. Two roulette wheels and a craps table are also open for instruction. At one of a half-dozen Blackjack tables, three Asian women in their forties are putting a fellow male student through his moves as a multi-deck dealer. The young man is almost ready to "audition" for Nick, the final test before formal certification. In his shorts, goatee, and Hawaiian shirt, Nick points to the young dealer's manicured nails. "It's like I'm their father," he says good-naturedly. "I tell them to get their hair cut and combed, to get shaved, to get cleaned up, get rid of your earrings, and hide your tattoos. The casinos want that wholesome all-American image."

Nick's rightfully jealous of his success rate and he doesn't want slovenly students to lower his stats. Three-fourths of his 600 enrollees per year finish his course and, he says, he's able to get at least 80 percent of them jobs right out of training. Where else in America, he asks, can you walk in off the street and, no matter what your background, train for a whole new career in Blackjack—a 100-hour course for only $249? Or add a second specialty in craps, roulette, baccarat, or poker for an extra couple of hundred bucks.

"I get some of the top 3 percent of the graduating class from UNLV," he says. "All they can show is a cubicle and maybe twenty-five grand a year for their four years of study. Let me give them four *weeks* of class and they can beat that all to hell," Nick says, citing several examples of students making a thousand dollars a week or more in their second year. "I have some kids who can crash this course in seven to ten days. They have no choice. They come out here with just enough to pay for three weeks rent and have to hit the road running."

Yet, walking around his academy and chatting with the students—young and old—I find anything but desperation. For the most part, the students seem to relish their practice as much as Ziggy does suiting up every night. It's as if those towering casinos nearby are rock-solid guarantees of a future. The bad news of the outside world—recession, stagnation, rising unemployment and declining wages—might be factors that got them here, but they somehow no longer figure very much in their future. For that mere $249 they've bought a foothold in the only niche of the American economy that grows no matter what. The only serious threat to their future stability, Nick says, is their own character and the siren call of the city that tempts them.

"Why does demand stay so high for jobs that are so good? Well, how hard do you think it is for a twenty-one-year-old kid to control this environment? Pretty damn hard," he says. "Drinking and gambling twenty-four hours a day all around you ain't easy. I tell them to hold on and stick it out because it's worth it."

"Another good thing about gambling I tell them," Nick continues. "Once you graduate here, nowadays you can go anywhere in America and work. You got your tools with you. And if you can say you've been trained in Vegas, well then, man, you're locked and loaded. You've got a future wherever you go."

As if on cue, Nick's 11 A.M. appointment walks into his office, a windowless backroom stuffed with books, trophies, and posters of Elvis, Corvettes, and the Scorsese movie, *Casino*.

The new prospective student is a burly, buffed, thirty-three-year-old clean-cut blond from Kansas I'll call Jim. He's been working night shift as a watchman at the Sun Coast casino northwest of the Strip. Nick quickly goes through his sales spiel, but Jim needs no convincing. After five minutes he's ready to sign and eagerly tells Nick he's planning to power through the course, coming three or four days a week, four or five hours a day. Nick tells him he will never regret this decision.

How could he? Jim's wife, Delia is standing next him to cradling their two-year-old son. A tall, twenty-eight-year-old black-haired knockout beauty in tight jeans and midriff showing off her rock-hard belly, Delia followed a former boyfriend out here from Florida five years ago. They broke up, she soon hit the skids and wound up working as a nude dancer at the Little Darlings club. That's where she met her current hubby, Jim, who was a club bouncer. "I don't know where I would have wound up if I stayed as a dancer," she says. Instead, a friend recommended Nick's school and three years ago she took the craps course. Now a dice dealer at the Flamingo, Nick figures she must make well over fifty thousand dollars a year. Maybe a lot more. "I love it so much," she says of her job. "I never thought I could be so happy," she says squeezing the chubby baby boy.

"As soon as he gets his first dealing job," she says putting the baby down and patting Jim's beefy shoulder, "we're gonna buy our dream house. I've already got it picked out." Nick asks her where, and soon there's an animated conversation filling the room over the relative merits of buying into either Summerlin, Green Valley, or out near Red Rock, the three hottest real estate markets in greater Las Vegas. The excitement that Jim and Delia palpably exude seems completely detached from the economic headlines, completely out of sync with what now seems the endless jobless recovery. They must be feeling something akin to what some of Henry Ford's line workers experienced when they could first afford their own Model T.

Andrea Hackett, of the Dancer's Alliance, meanwhile, has drifted into stormy waters. The wave of publicity her notoriety has generated is taking its toll. A cover story, focusing heavily on her personal life, just came out in a local alternative weekly. Although her unusual sexual history was never a secret, and she had mentioned it to several reporters including me, the *CityLife* cover is the first major local story to detail it. "The next day I walked into the Déjà Vu and after seven years the boss fires me on the spot," Andrea says one day over lunch at the gritty Pepper Mill, one of the last coffee shops on the Strip. "He said, 'Men come here to have *women* dance with them.' " Two days later she got another job at the lowest-end variety of dance clubs in a nearby strip-mall, but didn't make it through one shift before she was canned again. Fearing that she's being blackballed by club owners angry over her organizing efforts, rather than her sexual history, Andrea's down but not out. She says she's going ahead with efforts to secure some sort of affordable health insurance plan for Vegas dancers as to fill both an urgent need and to serve as a lure for joining the Alliance. And she's preparing complaints against both clubs that fired her with the National Labor Relations Board. For the moment, though she needs to find a job. And with the politically connected dance-club owners uniting against her, she knows it's not going to be easy.

Gambling Alone:
The Rise of the Machines

VANNA WHITE'S GETTING IMPATIENT waiting for me. Not quite sure what my next move will be, I've been standing idle too long. Too long for Vanna turns out to be about fifteen seconds. Her angelic visage frowns a bit, her moist lips tightening. "Come on," she says. "There's plenty of money to win. Press the button!"

Who can resist such solicitation? I dutifully press Vanna's button and the powerful AVP processor of the nine-foot-high, five-reel, fifteen-line, seventy-five-coin, Special Edition *Wheel of Fortune* video slot machine cranks into action, and some combination or another of letters falling together on its state-of-the-art nineteen-inch monitor has rewarded me with a free extra spin as the Wurlitzer-like Bonus Wheel on the top of the machine flashes and rings. Urged on once again by the irresistible Vanna, I push the play button again and win hundreds of credits that light up on a second screen with six reels, four rows, and twenty pay lines. Before I can even figure out what I've hit, the digital Dolby-doctored voice of Pat Sajak congratulates me on my win. Too bad I'm not playing with real money.

Standing next to me at the slot machine expo at the Rio Hotel and Casino, beaming as bright as the bonus wheel, is Ed Rogich. His brother, Sig, is Nevada's most powerful political consultant and king-maker, a former advisor to President George H.W. Bush. Ed also wields considerable power, but from a different vantage. He's vice-president of marketing for International Game Technology, IGT. Ed Rogich couldn't be happier if Vanna were there in the actual flesh giving us back massages. "Is this great? Or is it great? This is our top of the line," he says. "It's all about games," he says thoughtfully, caressing the towering, talking machine in front of us. "Look at the colors. We've gone from 256 colors to millions. It allows us to do real video streaming with no glitches. Real 3-D. Enhanced sound. The best animation. This is AVP—Advanced Video Project. This is the future. Here's Pat and Vanna talking to you—personally."

Well, not exactly just to me. More like talking to half of America. Slot machines are the motor force of modern gambling—accruing as much as 75 percent of the Vegas casino revenue. In 1989 there were 185,000 gambling machines in the U.S. Today there are nearly 750,000. Their cash take has increased from $11 billion to $40 billion over the same period. While some casinos guarantee the player a return of 95 percent, or even 99 percent on certain "designated" machines, most of the slots are fabulously profitable to the house, paying back much closer to the 75 percent minimum set by state law. Nor is there anything random about the rate of profit. Each machine's return rate is predetermined down to the decimal point by adjustable computer chips that are regularly spot-checked on the casino floor by roaming state gaming agents. The house takes no risks and can pretty much calculate just how much each machine will render on a yearly basis. Two identical machines can be set for radically different pay-outs to meet the market contours of two different casinos. And casinos, by the way, love the machines. They don't get sick, don't take coffee breaks, don't ask for maternity leave, don't even think about unionizing, and foot for foot constitute the most profitable use of valuable floor space.

It's Nevada-based IGT that boldly dominates this booming slot and video machine market, having minted 70 percent of the devices already in use world wide. The company, currently licensed in every gambling venue in the country, made $846 million from the 150,000 machines it sold in 2002 and another $882 million from leasing and profit-sharing agreements it has worked out with client casinos. "If we sold this machine," Rogich says, nodding toward Pat and Vanna, "it would run something like ten thousand dollars. But it's much more profitable for us to put it on a casino floor and split the revenues with the house."

And those revenues keep growing. While cutting edge machines like *Wheel of Fortune* allow play at as low a level as a nickel or even a penny, it can put seventy-five coins in play at a time. Play for a lowly quarter and you're risking nearly twenty bucks every ten or fifteen seconds. Described by IGT executives as the "pinball machines of the baby boom generation," the new computerized video betting machines have eased the shift in public image from gambling to gaming, ultimately to a form of TV watching. You're not really gambling so much as you're *playing*. The video machine revolution is the greatest destigmatization and massification of gambling in history, bringing millions of new gamblers into the market. Those who previously found table games, or even old-style one arm bandit slot machines to be too complicated, too intimidating, too sinful, or just too tainted by historic reputation, now find their wagering outlets in video machines. If Neil Postman's theory is at all correct—that TV-like entertainment values now dominate most of our social discourse and interaction—then these machines have moved gambling from the realm of the stogie-smokers to that of the mouse-clickers and channel-flippers.

"In this day and age our games have to be democratic," says Bill Thompson, one of UNLV's top gambling industry experts. "The yokel from Nebraska has got to have the same chance as the sharpie from L.A. We want the yokels to feel they have the same chance because we want those yokels here. And when that yokel walks into a casino and sees a complicated Blackjack table he goes 'Uggghhhh. I'm not gonna play *that*.' He's gonna play the machine. There is *no* skill required and they are very addictive."

The machine also appeals directly to the escape variety of gambler—the polar psychological opposite of the more social table gambler who seeks action and the adrenaline rush. Consistent with the trend of more and more Americans experiencing their leisure activity divorced from community, as Robert Putnam argues in his regarded *Bowling Alone,* machine gambling invites a TV-marinated public to enter one more individualized cocoon. "The number one fear of a compulsive video game player is that someone's going to sit down next to him and start talking," says Thompson. "Their number two fear is they win some sort of play that might give them back seventy-five coins but will take a minute or so for the machine to tote up. The player who's used to punching the button every eight seconds goes nuts."

Bill Friedman, who ran two successful casinos for the Hughes corporation, argues in his six-hundred-page *Designing Casinos to Dominate the Competition,* the most in-depth study of the subject, that the snugger, more isolating, more sealed-off, more confined a casino is, especially its machine gambling area, the more traffic and revenue it will produce. After conducting an exhaustive field study of just about every casino in the state, the former casino general manager and author came up with his list of successful "Friedman Principles:" The best casinos are "segmented . . . into separated gambling areas that create intimate playing settings." Players prefer gambling spaces with "short lines of sight" and with a "maze layout" that "creates many small, isolated, intimate playing areas."

Friedman also contends that low-ceiling joints beat out high-ceiling ones, that players prefer the "gambling equipment" as casino décor, rather than intricately themed interiors, and that a "compact, congested gambling-equipment layout" works more efficiently than a "vacant and spacious floor layout." The image of the perfect casino, evoked by Friedman's design studies, is one of a labyrinth of nooks and crannies inviting players, it seems, to curl up by themselves in front of their favorite machines, much as they do in front of the home TV—unmolested, unobserved and entranced.

But no matter how they're laid out on the casino floor, the strongest allure of the machines is that they demand nothing from the player—except constant feeding of coins. "Bottom line," says Thompson. "There aren't going to be any new games introduced here in Las Vegas that require much skill. If live table poker were just invented now, nobody would want it in the casinos. It's too complicated."

IGT's six hundred designers and engineers and those of

smaller companies like Bally's strain to match up new machines with the most recognized, most reassuring, least threatening themes and icons of American pop culture. The *Young Franken-stein* machine, explains an IGT marketing brochure, "stands out like a castle on a mountaintop" as the familiar recorded voice of Gene Wilder invites you to play its seventy-five coins at a time version. The *I Love Lucy* contraption offers up twelve lines of continuous play along with black-and-white video clips from the TV series. An optional spray feature, mounted atop the machine, douses the player in a homey, chocolate scent when the classic clip of Lucy bungling candies on a conveyor belt appears on the screen. The image and voice of Robin Leach accompanies players who try to match up animated yachts, limos, and mansions on the *Lifestyles of the Rich and Famous* machine; for those nostalgic for their elementary school passions there are the Uno and Magic 8-ball machines; the *Beverly Hillbillies* game pays out points in "moonshine money"; James Dean is reborn in the Diamond Cinema machine, as are long-buried and still gasping TV series in the *$10,000 Pyramid, Sale of the Century, Jeopardy, Family Feud, M.A.S.H,* and *Elvira— Mistress of the Dark* machines.

For macho types there are the Harley-Davidson slots. Beetle Bailey and Betty Boop open their slots for cartoon lovers. Austin Powers yells out "Yeah, baby" when a player wins on one of his video poker machines. For the more spicy-minded there's the five-reel, sixty-coins-at-a-time Tabasco hot-sauce machine with its "country store" bonus wheel and optional logo bottle-top piece. Also on the machine menu: Spam-themed slots. And if all this is still too complicated, then there's a plethora of childish, fully animated machines that have supplanted the classic cherries, plums, and oranges of yesteryear's three-reel mechanical

98% payback. Better than some 401 ks.

Venice in the desert.

Andrea Hackett: dancer and organizer.

Ziggy: master dealer.

Nick Kallos: dealer teacher.

3 a.m. gambling alone.

Benny Binion: Downtown's Rustler King.

Howard Schwartz: gambler's librarian.

The Big O.

Brother David Buer and his flock.

The wrong end of Fremont Street.

Competing with the casinos.

"What happens here, stays here."

Fading Glory: Bugsy's First Joint.

So many Elvi, so little time.

What Would Jesus Bet?

stepper slots with jumping and gyrating, singing and dancing bunny rabbits, chipmunks, squirrels, and piggies. The wildly popular and pernicously named Reel-Em-In game features, of course, squirming fishies. For blind players there's a machine with braille buttons and crooned tunes by Ray Charles. One series of slot machines pays off in real diamond chips. Other jackpots include $25,000 Chevies or $50,000 'Vettes. And the scorching-hot, network-linked megabucks jackpots can pay off, literally, in the tens of millions (though your odds of winning are less than one in fifty million).

Vintage-style, three-reel-steppers, the well-known one-armed bandits, the fruit-laden or Blazing-7 slots, remain quite popular and still account for more than half the machines in the Vegas casino market. The newest generation of these machines, in reality, are computer-driven, non-mechanical "mimics" of the older generation and are souped up with digital music and sound effects, "providing more entertainment and producing more seat-time," as one slot designer rather clinically tells me. You can pull the handle, if it makes you feel better, but there are no moving gears—the handle is connected to nothing except an electronic relay. The wheels will rotate just the same if you tap the lit-up "spin" button on the machine faceplate.

Some devotees play the slots, primarily video poker machines, "strategically." As in Blackjack, the video poker player exercises some degree of control and influence over the outcome and dedicated, skilled "computer perfect" players claim to squeeze considerable profits out of the "looser" machines. The "locals," the Vegas-based players, many of them casino employees and elderly retirees, are particularly fond of video poker and are known to be quite discriminating where they'll play. They studiously avoid the Strip casinos which they rightfully suspect are nothing but shake-down tourist joints stocked with stingy slots and they tirelessly shop the smaller, out-of-the-way casinos which house more generous, "looser" machines.

Video poker started out as a simple, straightforward game of five-card draw. But the newest poker machines are also being increasingly hyped up—and disadvantageously junked up—by the industry. At the Rio Hotel slot expo, IGT machine salesman Larry Del Mar shows off the latest of these dazzling creations, the downright devilish Multi-Strike Poker machine.

After a brief demonstration from Del Mar on how to play this sucker and after he tells me where the first prototypes of the machine have been deployed, I rush off to one of the favorite local casinos, the off-Strip Orleans, to hunt them down. After navigating an ocean of machines on the casino floor, I finally find the only bank of four Multi-Strike machines.

Breaking my conscientious objection to ever playing machines, and suspecting from the earlier demo session that this just might be the single most seductive, and sinister, gambling machine ever invented, and telling myself that, in any case, this is for research purposes, I let the Multi-Strike machine load itself up with twenty-five dollars worth of bills from my wallet. This machine plays twenty credits or "coins" at a time. So setting the machine for a dollar a coin seems absurdly high; even a quarter seems to pricey at this rate. Making sure no one is watching, I press the interactive screen and for the first time in my life opt for play at five cents. But times twenty, it's still a hefty buck-a-throw, five hundred credits in total to play with.

The insidious design of this machine is hardly covert. Play the maximum twenty coins and its internal computer gleefully and musically clicks out four exquisitely rendered hands of poker on four separate bands on the brightly colored screen. You've bet five coins on each hand. If you win the first hand the machine totes up your pay-out, and "escalates" you to the second hand. Win that hand and it fetchingly pays out at twice the normal schedule of odds and pushes you up to the third hand. Very sweet, because a win there pays out four times the normal amount. Make it to the top, and final, fourth hand, as I did on several occasions, and you can win a fat and juicy *eight* times the regular pay-out. I freely admit that each time I get bumped to the fourth round, and the digital, bassy *du-dah* resonates up my spine, visions of hitting a royal flush and netting thirty-two thousand credits race through my head—though no single hand ever pays me more than one hundred sixty nickels—eight bucks.

My original hunch was spot on. While most machines are numbing experiences, Multi-Strike is a thriller, as it frequently enough elevates me right to the brink of some fabulous jackpot. But its downside is a sledgehammer. Of the twenty coins bet each round, the machine places five on each of the four hands. If I win the first hand, my pay-out is based on the five-coin bet—which seems fair enough. But lose the first hand and, sorry sucker, you lose all twenty coins—an illogical and abusive outrage. I have no idea what the casino's mathematical edge is on such a game—but it can't be much less than if it slipped a vacuum hose into my pockets. I can only report on the concrete outcome. My first twenty-five dollars lasts me exactly twenty-eight minutes of nickel play. Making sure my research is solid, I invest another twenty-five dollars and that lasts me thirty minutes before I tap out. If I'd been playing at the modest 25-cent level, I would be losing $250 an hour. Or an even thousand dollars per hour at a dollar per credit rate. I ask the plumpish lady playing two machines over what she thinks of the new machine that she seems connected to. A curled, coiled lime-green plastic cord runs from around her neck to a small "players club" card that is plugged into the machine. "You lose quicker," she says. "But it's more fun."

What's better?

"If There's Anything
to Know about You . . ."

WALTZ ACROSS THE MACHINE-cluttered floor of just about any casino and, especially in the wee hours, it might appear to be a scene out of the camp Michael Douglas film, *Coma*. Clumps of near-lifeless bodies, seemingly suspended and transfixed in front of the video slots, and—like the woman next to me playing Multi-Strike—hooked up with bright coiled umbilical cords to the clanging machinery. The players club cards on the end of those cords might as well be their lifelines; they're often the principal reason, or at least the prevailing justification, for gambling in the first place.

Most players know very well that they are going to lose and, consequently, want something extra, something back for their sacrificial efforts. A full 50 percent of quarter-slot players tell researchers they expect to play for only one hour before busting out. A third of them think they will last two hours. Only 16 percent guess they will survive three hours. Most wind up playing much longer, and losing much more—the average Vegas gambling budget now floats near six hundred dollars per person, per trip. So much higher, then, the demand for casino comps, the freebie lures handed out to players.

But who's got whom by the tail?

The information on the magnetic strips on the back of those cards meld into highly sophisticated computer systems that track every move of the player. Play enough and long enough and—just as with an airline frequent flyer card—you "earn" comped meals and merchandise, or a dribble of cash back, or discounted rooms. Bet enough and the casino will only be too happy to "host" you with free rooms, gourmet meals, limos, and show tickets. Local players and frequent gamblers can as much as live off the freebies and the torrential flow of direct-mail casino promotions.

"Go to any retirement community here and watch the constant flow of casino shuttle buses running back and forth. Some casinos virtually adopt some of these folks," says prominent Vegas historian Eugene Moehring. "I had a couple of elderly neighbors who retired out here from New York, the husband had worked at Con Ed. They'd get up every morning early, get dressed and head right for the Stardust. She'd play slots all day and he played two dollar Blackjack. The casino comped them every meal. When he died, five dealers came to his funeral."

Staci Columbo, the perky business-suited V.P. of loyalty marketing for Vegas's "locals-oriented" Stations Casinos, says: "Our guests become very reliant on our monthly packages. We know for a fact that our regular customers use OfficeMax calendars and lay out our coupons for each day of the month. So we customize our offers to make it friendly to the calendaring process."

None of this stems from management largesse, but rather from what's called "the science of decision-oriented prediction."

The goal is not only to maximize customer "seat-time," but also to increase REVPAC—Revenue Per Available Customer. The formula is simple enough. Seeking brand loyalty, most casinos are willing to "comp" back about 40 percent of the estimated player win. Their win, that is. Your loss.

Comping is an old Vegas tradition. "The man with the pencil" was the pit boss or floor man that could, at will and by the seat of his pants, write up a freebie ticket for whatever he thought was necessary to make you happy. But that system has gone the way of personalized banking, shoved aside by cold, computerized databanking and analysis systems replete, even, with ATM-like card readers that in some casinos allow players to see a running "balance" of their earned points.

My first brush with a players' club came in 1993 as I checked into the fading Tropicana for a weekend stay. As I completed the registration card, the clerk handed me a pre-prepared Island Winners Club card with my name embossed in gold. If I played five-dollar Blackjack for a minimum of four hours per day and made sure I handed the card to the dealer at each sitting, I was told, my room charge of eighty-nine dollar per night would be comped. At the end of the weekend, those eight hours of play cost me more than three hundred dollars—but the room fee was waived. Today, the loyalty clubs are far more extensive and complicated.

Born in Atlantic City casinos in the early '80s, only the technological revolution of the last decade has allowed the so-called players clubs to fully flower. Now virtually every casino with more than a few dozen slots and a handful of card tables struggles to enlist and enroll every player who walks through the door into its own club.

But the comp system is no indiscriminate blunderbuss. No national shortage of casino gamblers plagues the industry. On the contrary, over the last decade, among households that gamble, the allotment for "gaming" has risen from 9 percent to 17 percent of the disposable budget. "But casinos have figured out that 80 percent of their business comes from the best 20 percent of their customers," says marketing professor and industry consultant, Stowe Shoemaker. "These programs don't necessarily get you to gamble more as much as they get you to concentrate it in one place."

And Shoemaker and just about every other industry expert agree that no single corporation more effectively deploys loyalty marketing strategies than Harrah's—a gambling giant with more than two dozen casinos across the country and that is thought to spend as much as seventy million dollars a year on technology and high-tech research. Using a closed-loop, nationwide computer network, Harrah's samples and compiles customer information from its slot machines, gaming tables, call centers, hotel registration desks and, of course, from its employees. "The Harrah's guys are the real propeller heads," says Shoemaker. "They come straight out of the credit-card industry."

Indeed, if one man could alone embody the New Las Vegas, the corporate-bottom-line Vegas of prediction science, it's Harrah's Vice President of Total Rewards, Randy Fine. Pale, pudgy, ruddy-skinned, with close-cropped and sharply trimmed hair, Fine wears a button-down shirt, a sober, pin-striped navy-blue banker's suit, and peers through thick-lensed glasses. In his mid '30s, his pedigree is a Harvard MBA. Any mysterious back-street allure that some of us romantics might still associate with gambling quickly withers under a barrage of Fine's sure-fire, hard-nosed marketing calculations. He speaks so quickly, so self-assuredly of Harrah's customer strategy, that I struggle to keep up with him. He emphasizes how highly prized and how tightly targeted is that potential maximum Revenue Per Available Customer:

> "We *don't* do blanket, monthly offers to our club members. Some might get seven or eight mailings a month, some might get none. . . . People get offers based on their predictive behavior or on their past record and we tightly segment our offers to drive behavioral change . . . Our offers come from our database of twenty-five million customers. We have a world-class [computer] system that tells us if we should give a customer a room and at what price. This has driven up our gaming revenue 50 to 60 percent. And it's not just a bi-modal experience. Our problem isn't just filling a hotel, but with *whom* we fill it. We want the best players, the players who are going to give us the best revenue while staying in that room. So when a [players' club member] calls us, we know right away to tell them we have a room for them or that we don't, or that it's free or available at some other rate.
>
> What we want to avoid is a simple incremental expense in giving that room. So if we can get someone to shift a trip from a loaded Saturday to a Tuesday, that's a win for us. We've opened a valuable room for a higher-stakes player.
>
> Our system allows so that every customer who calls us gets a unique answer in sixty seconds. In real time our system is calculating our hotel capacity, how we want to fill the hotel, and who you are. You get an answer right away. We have twenty years of data on the same people.
>
> We know everything about you; what you play; how much you play; when you play. We have people at Harrah's

who love numbers *a lot!* So much, that they collect numbers on everything and everybody before they even have a friggin' idea of what we're gonna do with those numbers. In short, if there's anything to know about you, we're gonna know it."

The computerization of casino comping has, in one sense, made things more democratic. Like redeeming those old blue chip stamps, anyone who participates in a players club gets something back, even if it's just a token reward. But the personal touch has been lost. "Real service went out with the mob," says long time pit man Kenny Franks. "The mob gave service because they were mostly illiterate and the only way *they* got service was with their bankroll. So they understood by their own experience what it meant to be treated right."

"Back then the casino was king," Franks says. "It gave the orders, and everything else was a giveaway. Go to a show and two-thirds of the guests were comped. A player needed something? OK. The casino would call over to the restaurant and say 'Send this guy what he wants—three steaks, two bottles of champagne and, yeah, that opium pipe he was asking about.' And the restaurant would say 'Yes, sir!' But after the corporations came in, not just the casino, but *every* aspect of the operation now has to make a profit. The other night I was playing poker over at the Palms and they brought in a couple of boxes of donuts for the players from the outside. I overheard the casino people fighting with the food people as to who was gonna get charged for the bill."

The newest trend in casino technology are computer programs that go far beyond just archiving how much a client has gambled. According to a recent report in *Gaming Today* ("News You

Can Bet On") new "data warehousing" software takes information not only from the casino floor, but also from the front desk, hotel restaurants, and from the players club cards and instantaneously merges and integrates it into an intimately detailed individual profile. The same software tracks hold—or win—percentages on every table and machine, the popularity of different types and brands of slots, and allows casino management to "see," in real time, from a single monitoring computer which machines slot players are frequenting or shunning. From the central computer, casino managers can track up-to-the-second playing and betting patterns of an individual player and can immediately dispatch "hosts" to rush over and offer them comps, rewards, and freebies.

The Vegas-based Compudigm company sells a technology called "seePOWER" that features thermographic, on-screen readouts of casino hot spots. For the first time, casino bosses can exploit a visual, graphic representation of the entire gaming floor. Among the clients that are serviced through a distribution system run by IGT is Harrah's Entertainment. "Over time, you can see what is happening on the slot floor," Compudigm senior sales manager Lydia Wohlwerth tells *Gaming Today*. "The redder the heat, the more activity you have, or the more coins you have in."

What better way to instantly track promotions and come-ons? "You can measure the play down to the group," Wohlwerth boasts. "You can look for females thirty-five to forty who come in on Saturday between 5 and 7 P.M. with a thirty-mile drive time. You can measure the impact on your business depending on who you've marketed to. We have clients who have abandoned traditional marketing to this approach."

Speeding up the flow of cash into the slots is the next great expanding frontier in machine gambling. Already 10 percent of gambling machines nationwide are "cashless"—no more messy—and slow—feeding of coins or rumpled bills into the hungry mouths of the slots. "Ticket-in-ticket-out" systems are quickly gaining ground. Now the loyal customer, anxious to get the machine reels spinning, can buy a predetermined amount of credit on a computerized card, which works the same way a long distance phone card does. When he wants to cash out, there are no more coins to scoop up and jangle in a cottage-cheese container. Instead, the slot machine prints out a voucher that can be redeemed at the cashier cage.

"If this catches on, which isn't for sure yet, every casino's going to make x-amount more just because it's going to save all that time that now goes into changing coins," says one Stardust casino slot worker. "And think about this. How many people are going to decide that it's too much a pain in the ass to stand in the cashier's line to redeem a ticket that's worth only a buck or two? Multiply that by the thousands and thousands and that's that much more the casinos are gonna win."

"That Room"—Addicted

Bo Bernhard, the rising wunderkind of gambling research, meets me in the casino laboratory on the bottom floor of UNLV's International Gaming Institute at the William F. Harrah College of Hotel Administration. Courses and seminars in gaming development, gaming management, surveillance, casino auditing, detection of cheating, gaming preparation—and many others—are regularly taught in this spacious room equipped with sixteen blinking slot machines, a half-dozen varied gaming tables stocked with cards, shoes, and chips, and a state-of-the-art Eye-in-the-Sky system all wired up and ready to go overhead.

It's got to be the only university gambling lab in the world. And Bo, with undergraduate honors degrees in psych and sociology from Harvard and with a PhD in the latter, and who at barely age thirty holds the titles of "Director of Gambling

Research" and "Assistant Professor of Hotel Management and Sociology," has agreed to me meet me here after I heard mention of the place. Bo, who got his doctorate in 2002 for his sociological history of problem gambling, says he, and others, occasionally use the lab as they investigate player reaction to gaming—the physical and social interaction among gamblers. "For some people," he says, "something like the Fourth of July is going off in their brains as they gamble."

Understanding gambling, gamblers, and especially problem gamblers drives Bo's work. And it's a tough field because, as he and most of his colleagues agree, just as in the field of sex research, people often just don't tell the truth about their relationship to gambling. "When you poll people on the phone about gambling, can you trust *anything* they say? No population offers more research challenges than gamblers. And I admit, studying gambling may sound goofy," he says "but if you're not studying this, then you are not studying what moves the masses."

Whatever the ambiguities of just who gambles how much and when, some certainties nevertheless arise from modern research. "It's trendy to say gambling is sweeping America," Bo says. "But mostly it's machine gambling that's sweeping America. And these machines are a convergence of so many factors: the logic of capitalism, technology, and increasing comfort with machines."

Robert Putnam has a paragraph in *Bowling Alone* where he comments that casino attendance is one of the few social activities still on the rise in America. But for most problem gamblers, gambling becomes a solitary activity. "Today's gambling environment is much less social than yesteryear's gambling halls and saloons. What we're really seeing is what I call a 'deforestation' effect—the machines quickly overtaking and crowding out everything else on the floor," he says.

As someone who was born and raised in Vegas, and like hundreds of thousands of other residents here who never gamble, and as a researcher who investigates all aspects of gambling, Bo takes extra caution in underlining that gambling, even frequent gambling, doesn't necessarily indicate any sort of problem or addiction. Some people can gamble every week or every day and not have a problem. Others may hit the casinos only once a month but still be captive to a pathology. But for those who are hooked, Bo says, the rise of the machines has radically altered the profile of the gambling addict. "The result is often a very lifelike, beepin' and boppin' machine sitting in front of a very zombie-like, machine-like player," he says.

"On the one hand, gambling has become the great American pastime. Like it or not, this is now what we do in our leisure time and it's here to stay," Bo says as we retreat from the lab to his upper-floor, book-laden office. "But it can also be a sickness. And yet, addicts are still more stigmatized than understood."

Through its publicly funded university system, Nevada teaches just about every imaginable facet of gambling and casino management, including for-credit field trips to casinos. But, to the ongoing amazement of many the state of Nevada doesn't spend as much as a dollar on treating problem gamblers. It doesn't fund a single treatment program or service. For the second year in a row, the Nevada legislature refused to even consider a proposed bill, one lobbied for by Bo and others, that would have allocated at least a paltry $250,000 to gambling addiction treatment. But, as they say, tough luck buddy.

By contrast, Louisiana, with only a few legal casinos, earmarks four million dollars for dealing with gambling addicts.

Even Iowa, that allows operation of less than a handful of small riverboat casinos, spends more than $2.5 million a year on the issue. The Vegas gambling industry, the casinos that take in nearly ten billion dollars a year in revenue, do fund some smaller research and "educational" programs on problem gambling, but the total amount spent could probably be financed by the yearly take of a single row of a dozen slot machines. The Harrah's corporation recently rolled out a nationwide ad campaign urging Americans to gamble only "responsibly." A nice side effect, if not indeed the intended primary effect of the campaign, according to a recent study by Harrah's is that where the ads were test marketed, the brand name recognition of Harrah's increased from 28 percent to 40 percent.

Not surprisingly, many of the casino industry–backed addiction studies estimate that just over 1 percent of the American population has a gambling problem. More independent studies put the figure as possibly being much higher. One recent poll by Gemini Research concluded that almost 6 percent of Nevadans might be problem or pathological gamblers. There's also little agreement on the social cost of problem gambling in the Vegas area. Industry lowball estimates float at around twelve million dollars a year. On the other extreme, other studies suggest that Southern Nevada suffers a much higher toll.

Wherever the economic truth resides, the human cost is undeniable and immediately visible (except, of course, by Nevada state government). Any way you stack the stats, tens of thousands of problem gamblers live in the Vegas area. Many of them are the elderly, who have little other activity. And many of them are young.

"There are plenty of seniors of our greatest generation," Bo

Bernhard says, "who have budgeted their whole lives, and even now as they are retired and gamble even regularly, they still stick strictly to their budgets. There are also plenty of seniors who are recreational gamblers, who have nothing else to do, but still keep it under control. But for me, personally, the problem stories I hear from both seniors and from Gen-X'ers are the hardest to deal with." Bo's brow furrows with emotion. He catches me catching him and he adds with a tension-relieving laugh: "I guess that's why I'm a failed clinician."

In some ways, it's odd happenstance that Bo has committed his work and study to the gaming industry and especially problem gambling. His great-great maternal grandfather, known as Kid Jordan, got kicked out of Texas for running illegal gambling joints and came to Vegas in the great hustler migration of the '30s—right after Nevada legalized gambling. The paternal side of Bo's family moved to Vegas as part of the military job boom of World War II. His grandfather worked at the Nuclear Testing Site. "The family joke was that his job was that he'd go out and check the dead animals after the tests," Bo says. "What isn't a joke is that he died of cancer."

"But like so many Las Vegans," he says, "my family has gone from a shady past to the mainstream. From Kid Jordan to a family full of teachers. My grandmother was one of the founders of Head Start in Las Vegas. Her husband was the principal of one of Las Vegas's first desegregated schools."

He says, contrary to the popular image of Vegas as a conservative cowboy town, his parents were "liberal hippie types." His mother taught human growth development at community college. Bo's father, an attorney, the former head of the State Ethics Commission, is today chair of the Nevada Gaming Commission, the gambling regulatory agency.

It's because of this richly textured and hybrid background that Bo, more than any other Vegas academic I have met, is the most unyieldingly demanding in precisely delineating the realities from the myths of Las Vegas and Vegas gambling. "My relationship to gambling, as a youngster growing up in Vegas, was nonexistent," he says. "We went to L.A. all the time and I just assumed that all those skyscrapers were full of slot machines. Meanwhile, my parents never gambled. I saw my Dad drop a couple of quarters once into a slot machine at a 7-11. But that's all I remember.

"But I spent *so* much of my youth answering stupid questions— like if my mother was a dancer or my father a dealer. So, if you grow up here, you enter into this place where you get defensive— trying to explain to people that you are normal, that you go to public school, to church, and that you play little league. I've lived all over the world, and everywhere I have gone, when I said was from Las Vegas, I knew what was coming next: instant mistaken assumptions."

After graduating from his local high school in 1991 and being accepted to Harvard, Bo assumed it was "signed, sealed, and delivered" that he would eventually go into law and stay on in Boston. But his voracious intellectual curiosity and honed liberal instincts drew him into both psychology and sociology, in which he double-majored. There was still no inkling, however, that his study would come full circle back to his hometown industry of gambling. Not until, in his upper division years, he found himself being mentored, rather counterintuitively, by conservative sociologist Richard Herrnstein, author of the controversial *The Bell Curve*. As Herrnstein was dying, he urged Bo to apply his studies to what he knew best, the world of Las Vegas gambling.

Taking up the challenge, Bo began meeting with Dr. Robert Hunter, the dean of problem gambling treatment in Vegas. And though his mentor, Richard Herrnstein, had become a darling of American conservatives, Bo still retained his own opposing ideological view. "My first instinct was to want to go back to Vegas and *prove* from my politically liberal perspective that problem gambling was, in fact, a myth. That it was one more invention of the Christian Right, one more moralistic attack on popular culture."

"But then," he says reflectively, "but then, Dr. Hunter took me into *that room* one Thursday night and that was it. I never stopped coming back. I saw many things in that room. I saw many truths in that room. I saw a friend in that room. I saw my work in that room. I went into that room and I never stopped coming back."

Bo doesn't need to tell me what room he's talking about. A few weeks earlier, on a different Thursday night, and as a special favor, he had also taken me there. And he also knew that I was as moved as he was the first time he had been let in.

"The room" is but a bare-walled, thinly carpeted, air-conditioned rectangle with none of the machines or tables that line the UNLV casino lab. Instead, about twenty chairs are pushed against its four walls. Shuttered windows on one side of the room open on a parking strip. This is the meeting room of the Problem Gambling Center, the PGC, the one and only nonprofit gambling addiction treatment center in Las Vegas—for that matter, in the entire state of Nevada. And, not so coincidentally, it is one of the few state institutions, public or private, that has the word "gambling"—rather than "gaming"—in its title.

An otherwise unremarkable collection of small, fluorescent-lit offices in a nondescript office park, the PGC gets even less public notice or attention than the languishing exhibitions at Fort Mormon. About 90 percent of its anemic $170,000 annual budget comes from casino industry contributions. The state sees fit to contribute nothing. With intensive peer counseling, classic behavioral therapy, focused self-evaluation, and close cooperation with Gamblers Anonymous—which has a meeting somewhere in Las Vegas on just about every hour of the week—the PGC treats about 140 clients a year and claims about a 70 percent rate of success.

Thursday nights are group self-evaluation meetings— intimate, soul-baring sessions into which outsiders are rarely allowed. But Dr. Robert Hunter, who still runs the center, is convinced that at least occasionally letting a reporter in will help get his message out that gambling addiction is mostly an overlooked and under-attended sickness.

Dr. Hunter, tall and fair-complexioned, wearing blue jeans, scuffed work boots, and a faded polo shirt, emits the kind of crackling nervous energy that is, doubtless, a minimum prerequisite for keeping such a beleaguered and shoe-string operation still humming.

Twenty years ago or so, both Bo and Dr. Hunter tell me, the profile of the average problem gambler was a cigar-chomping action gambler, a card player or dice shooter, relentlessly searching for the big wins and jackpots. "That's a disappearing breed," says Hunter, as we chat before the group session gets underway. "Today the problem gambler is likely to be a thirty-four-year-old woman with two kids and two years of college. And a video game addiction. We're not seeing many of the dinosaur action gamblers who play to feel a rush. We're seeing people who say they want to feel numb, want to blank out, want to lose track. It's hard to imagine what an intoxicant it can be for them."

As tonight's group begins to drift in, Hunter introduces me to one of his clients who has just come in. An attractive, highly educated professional in her late thirties, Sue is elegantly dressed right down to her crocodile shoes. Diamonds and gold sparkle from her ears and fingers. Her blonde hair is expertly and expensively coiffed. Her southern drawl is cultured and mannered. Her temper is upbeat and cheerful. She's been off the machines now for twenty-two days and it is with surprising humor that Sue tells me of her descent into addiction:

I moved here about five years ago when I got married. Before that I never played poker, I had no interest in gambling, nothing. One day, in 1998, just to fool around, I sat down and hit four aces on a video poker machine and won $500. That was it.

What do I get out of it? Oh man, I get to disappear, it allows me to escape my world. It stimulates my mind. I become hyper-focused on patterns I think I'm detecting.

It began to be a problem a year after I started playing. From my own professional work I already knew a lot about addiction. I had lost maybe a hundred dollars a day playing Blackjack for a couple of weeks. So I figured, how much could I possibly lose just playing video poker for quarters? Well, the answer turned out to be $200 to $800 a day— sometimes $1,800. In the middle of all this, I inherited some money so I moved up from quarter machines to dollar machines. Toward the end, I was playing six or seven hours a day every Friday and every weekend.

I knew it was getting worse when I felt all I wanted

was more and more playing time. The first couple of times I hit a four-thousand-dollar jackpot, I'd go out and shop at Neiman Marcus or buy a piece of art. But I knew I was in trouble when I'd hit one of those jackpots and say to myself: "Oh, good. Now I've got enough money to gamble through the weekend." I quit, really, because I felt I was going to kill myself. I've got seventeen years of recovering from alcohol and not once did drinking make me think about suicide, nor did it create the financial and marital chaos that gambling has. To be honest, I had to quit because I just couldn't stand myself any longer. I figure in the last three years I lost more than two hundred thousand dollars in the machines.

Sue is among the ten women and six men who finally assemble in "the room" for their weekly group session. I sit next to Dr. Hunter at one end. Bo Bernhard sits facing us. In between are sixteen very normal, and seemingly very shell-shocked and visibly sad people—mostly middle-aged, but a few elderly and a few who are younger. I don't know their ages, or real names or their jobs. But by their looks, these are predominantly working-class and middle-class average-looking Americans. Dr. Hunter kicks off the session by asking all to briefly introduce themselves and say a few words about how they feel, saying, "Gamblers are masterful actors, adept at masking what they are really feeling."

Those who have been in treatment longer—four, five weeks—sound the steadiest. The newbies sound as shaken as Bo's grandfather might have been the first time he was told to rummage through an atomic dumping ground. "I'm Anthony," says one fortyish man in a white shirt and tie. "I feel kind of worried about my bills coming in, about how I'm going to get through all this. My last bet was thirty-seven days ago."

Dr. Hunter, like a skilled magician who knows every card in the deck, has a reassuring comeback line immediately ready to pull out for just about every response he hears. "Don't worry, Alex," he says. "You got a big raise thirty-seven days ago."

Another woman, calling herself Catherine, says, after five years of trying, she finally quit four days ago. "You still look haunted, honey," Hunter says, in a blaring understatement. Catherine looks like someone who has just glimpsed some unspeakable horror. "It'll start getting better next week, trust me," Hunter reassures her.

Sylvia, a husky working-class woman in her early thirties, her voice cracking, says that after maxing out both her credit cards at the Mandalay Bay she has no idea where she'll get the seven thousand dollars she needs to get her broken-down car fixed and brought back from New Mexico. Chris, a middle-aged Asian woman with a designer purse in her lap, says she's feeling "embarrassed, angry, sad, and ashamed."

"Lancing a boil is painful but necessary," Hunter responds. "And eventually it heals."

When it comes to Gerry's turn, she breaks out crying before any words come out. A rough-hewn woman in her mid-fifties, maybe with some Native American or Latina heritage, with close-cropped hair, and wearing jeans and a sweatshirt, it takes her a few moments to regain her composure. "I'm Gerry and I'm a compulsive gambler. And sorry to tell you, but I'm a failure. I was on my way to a [Gamblers Anonymous] meeting this afternoon and I never made it." Only on her third day of abstinence, she blew twenty bucks worth of quarters in a video machine when she stopped for a cold drink at a convenience store.

Hunter masterfully takes this painful anecdote and turns it into a moment of mirth and encouragement. "Honey," he says, "you haven't been in treatment long enough to relapse. Everyone slips sooner or later. But you'll be OK. The fact you are even telling us this makes you stronger."

Only once over the course of the next hour does Hunter ever depart from this embracing tone. Fuji, a soft-spoken woman of about forty-five, complains that she's feeling "confused" and mixed up. "I've tried this so many times before and it didn't work," she says forlornly. "I mean I really want to quit gambling. But do I? Do I want to stop gambling? Or do I just want to stop losing?"

Hunter shows some visible impatience and decides to switch to a tough-love approach, taking advantage of Fuji's ambivalence to deliver a mini-sermon.

"Don't tell me it's a pain in the ass to get here, goddamnit!" he says with his voice slightly rising. "You had *no* problem getting somewhere to gamble! No problem spending your kids' money! No problem waiting in line to play a machine!"

"Addiction is chronic and progressive," Hunter continues, his tone flattening back out and his eyes scanning the whole group. "But for your purposes right now you must realize you are addicted to gambling and if you continue it can kill you. Alcoholics can take twenty years to bottom out. Gambling addicts can do it in two years. There's no stronger addiction than gambling. It's not about the substance. It has nothing to do with the money. But it's about where it takes you. This is more about addiction than compulsion. Compulsion screws up your life. Addiction ends your life. You don't gamble like Tiger Woods compulsively practices golf. Goddamnit, you gamble like junkies shoot dope. Yet I know people who quit shooting dope because it got in the way of their gambling!"

The session ends with Bo taking the floor and smoothly leading a fifteen-minute question-and-answer session based on his ongoing research. The lively debate quickly turns to whatever differences there might be between compulsion or addiction and whether or not there's a physiological basis for gambling addiction. But by now I'm drifting in my own thoughts and emotions, and don't follow the give-and-take very closely.

Bo had told me earlier in the day that witnessing these sort of sessions might change forever the way I see gambling. Maybe. But watching these crushed people tell their wrenching stories certainly marks the way I now understand addicted gamblers. They are not fools, but rather victims. And I feel absolutely swamped by their profound sadness. I have an overwhelming sense of their having been cheated out of a chunk of their lives.

Perhaps it's too fine a distinction I make and, in the end, one more rationalization for the sort of gambling that I choose. But I remember my Aunt Lena who died about twenty years ago. Poorly educated, saddled with a deeply dysfunctional and recluse husband who refused to work, along with a brood of kids prone to drug addiction and petty crime, Lena fed them all, bailed them out, and barely scratched by, waitressing into her old age in low-pay greasy spoons. On two different occasions in the middle of her life, her husband's wealthy relatives handed down sizeable inheritances. And both times, Lena quit her job, dragged her husband out of his room, and spent weeks and months drinking and dancing, but mostly playing the horses until all the money was gone and she was back slinging hash.

Who knows what she was feeling inside. But she'd always claim to have no regrets, that the few months of affluence and abandon were worth it all, and that she'd always have great memories to rake through. Get her talking at any Thanksgiving family gathering, and she'd excitedly recall this or that race at Santa Anita or Hollywood Park, or the trifecta she hit on a certain afternoon at the Caliente track just across the Mexican border. She'd remember every detail, down to the jockey's colors, and could almost re-narrate the announcer's call of the race.

In the darkness of my car I ask myself what these tormented people I've just been with in the PGC have to show for their sacrifices. What, other than maybe a whiff of chocolate spray from the *I Love Lucy* machine, will they have to show for those entire livelihoods that have been smashed into thousands of quarter-sized shards?

Alone in that darkness I also ask a question that fills me with dread but now becomes unavoidable. What if anything do I have in common with them? I reassure myself that, give or take a few hundred dollars, and thankfully only a few hundred, I can stick within determined budgets; that what I spend on gambling—less than on some other costly hobbies I've honed—has no significant impact on my financial stability; and that, at least, like my departed Aunt Lena, I get a kick from the rush and can gamble, relatively, guilt free. At least until tonight. Maybe that will also change now.

That said, I'd be lying if I didn't admit that at least at some level, to some degree, I do know what those sixteen people in that room were feeling all those times they couldn't stand up from the machine and walk away. Maybe I could describe it this way. I've never been inside the psychological cages and cells that have trapped them. But I've been close enough to those cold iron bars that tonight, in the black solitude of the PGC parking lot, they send an icy shudder through my heart.

Baghdad Blackjack

VEGAS ISN'T BIG ON wars—they tend to be a terribly distracting drag on profits. And the war in Iraq is no different. Apart from the garishly opportunistic flashes of red-white-and-blue on a few of the hotel and casino billboards, it's obvious that Vegas would like the whole three-week-old Battle for Baghdad to just be over with and disappear. Yes, the Paris Hotel and Casino has dutifully taken down the traitorous French tricolor that usually flaps over its down-to-the-detail replica of the Acadamie Nationale de Musique. And the supposedly liberal-minded Hard Rock casino—which at one time designated a small portion of profits from three special slot machines to groups "saving the rain forest"—has, at least temporarily, stopped serving French wines in its restaurants and bars.

But that's about it. No one has yet suggested that the imported games of roulette and baccarat be renamed the Wheel of Empire or American Bluff. That's why I'm surprised that the one giant-sized TV monitor Binion's Horseshoe keeps lit in its relatively small, family-run downtown casino stays tuned to CNN and its round-the-clock war coverage, albeit with the sound muted. A few of the customers around me loudly grumble, asking the pit bosses to tune back to the usual sports fare of ESPN. But most of the players—at this hour of about 3 A.M. on the nineteenth or twentieth day of the war—concentrate on the cards in front of them and rather blithely ignore the news channel's colorful bottom-of-the-screen tickers and bumpers as they report: "Chemical Ali's body found . . . Saddam and two sons may be killed in air strike . . . Mosul pounded by waves of B-52s." They pay no attention to the kaleidoscopic footage of the desperate townsfolk of Basra scrambling and jostling for food and water, or the replay of U.S. marines toppling that big Saddam statue. A throaty chorus of cheers, whistling, and clapping suddenly erupts about twenty yards down to my right—but that's because someone's just made his or her point at the dice table and won big for everybody hanging over the side.

This is what Vegas is about. Tuning out the real world. Fifty years ago, the front-man owner of the Desert Inn, Wilbur Clark, told the *New Yorker* that the initial surge of tourist curiosity around the open-air A-bomb test shots that were rowdily celebrated at his Sky Room bar, very soon waned into indifference. "Around shot time the play in our casino seemed to go up and the drinking got heavier," Clark said. "The curious thing was the guests would drive here from Los Angeles to see a shot and then not bother to look at it. I'd instruct my pitmen to let the players at their tables know when it was about time for the flash, but the players would go right on with their games."

That's more or less what I'm doing—ignoring the war and

straining to stay afloat in a prolonged but steadily sinking match of hand-pitched, single-deck Blackjack. I suppose soldiers feel the same way, but with much more in play and at stake. "In the infantry, your only world is six inches in front of your nose," director and Vietnam vet Oliver Stone said to me shortly after he made *Platoon*. Right in front of my nose is the twenty-one game that Binion's offers at almost all of its tables—the nearest thing to pure, player-friendly Blackjack. And playing as attentively and carefully as I am, whittling down the already negligible house advantage, this game should have about dead-even odds.

So what? Nothing I do is working. I might as well be standing in a wheat field right under a wave of those thundering B-52s. Or maybe I should be playing with that special Pentagon deck of cards carrying the sinister visages of the Ba'ath. Maybe plopping down a Saddam of Spades will spook out the dealer.

Over the last three hours I've surrendered back just about all of the almost fifteen hundred dollars I won last month at the Mandalay Bay in that supposedly more shaved and unfair game of multi-deck. Winning that was luck. And tonight the Lady's extracting her payback. The middle-aged guy playing next to me only aggravates matters. He's neglecting to hit his high cards against dealer pat hands, taking cards when he should stay, and wildly over-betting. Whenever he screws up, it seems I lose. But then again, I'm losing just about every hand.

The masters of professional Blackjack, like Stanford Wong, counsel to pay no attention. A stupid player at your table, they say, in no way affects your outcome. Whatever mistakes he makes, he doesn't "throw off" the deck. The deck was random before and after he plays. That's true. But the game is stressful enough and having a haphazard or bone-headed player next to me is always an irritant. They are in-flesh reminders of how stupid any player can be, of how much the entire casino industry banks on that stupidity, and, ultimately, how stupid I might be for sitting there next to him.

Tonight I'm also battling back an unusual guilt attack. Not just over blowing my winnings, but also because as hard as I might try otherwise, I'm also zoning out on the war that's unfolding on the screen right in front of me. But the cards are, indeed, a powerful intoxicant. The still photo of Saddam Hussein and his two sons—Uday and Qusay, with their wavy hair and black mustaches—that CNN keeps reposting, appear in my faltering consciousness as three jacks. Or are they kings? CNN carries an Al-Jazeera story that U.S. forces have fired on a media building and that one, maybe two reporters are thought dead. I might even know the victims. I had been in Iraq on the eve of the first Gulf War and a few weeks ago I had the chance to cover Bush's rematch as an embedded reporter but couldn't carve out the time. If I had, I could have been in that building now being shelled. And now, with colleagues possibly under fire, I somehow can't make the time to walk away from the table and pay more attention to the story.

In reality, I'm not sure there's very much I could do about the war in Iraq if I weren't playing cards. I've performed my journalistic duty and published more than a few columns critiquing its rationale and probable outcome. But whatever guilt or remorse about gambling, or at least about losing, that I've previously repressed or side-stepped has found its excuse to boil upward tonight. Combine that with this jagged-edged losing streak, the images of the gambling addicts at the PGC fresh in my head, and it all adds up to something quite distasteful. At exactly 5 A.M., my previous month's winnings beaten down to only two hundred dollars, I resignedly give up the seat at

Binion's. Before I turn away, I see an American armored convoy gunning through Baghdad, a group of Iraqis staring on impassively from the sidewalks.

These are the most difficult, really excruciating sort of moments. What next? This is when I am tempted to make all the wrong moves. To sit down at another table and double my basic bet. To throw strategy out the window and start playing hunches. Or worse, I might head for the roulette table and try to make it all back in two or three lucky spins, betting my social security number, my wife's birthday, or my IQ, which at this hour would fit easily on the wheel's betting table which reaches no higher than thirty-six.

Or I might be desperate enough to pay attention to the three-foot-high LED read-out next to each wheel; a lit-up, rolling scoreboard that displays the last fifteen numbers that have come up. Every spin of the roulette wheel exists independently in time, having no correlation with previous spins. There is absolutely no history in roulette, the real odds on any number coming up is the same every time the ball drops. No number or color is ever "due" or "bound" to hit. But a dozen or so years ago, someone in the business had the brainstorm of installing those LED scoreboards and, with customers now seeing whatever patterns they thought they saw in the read-outs, revenue at the wheels immediately jumped twenty percent.

I could also decide to chase after my money by sitting down at the Caribbean Stud Poker table. Delightfully entertaining, and mercifully s-l-o-w, it is the only casino game where the player is punished if the dealer has a very good hand *or* a very bad one. Only something in between can really let you win. In the meantime, you have to literally rent space at the table, paying a dollar per hand to be included in the fabulously lucrative progressive jackpot that rewards the one-in-a-million authentic royal flush.

I boldly forego all these temptations and, instead, rather self-righteously, opt for breakfast at the all-night, unreconstructed '50s Liberty Diner inside the White Cross pharmacy a mile or so south toward the Strip, smack-dab in the edgy, tenebrous no-man's land around the Stratosphere casino. The Liberty Diner—some, including me, think—might just be the best greasy spoon in America. But you taste its wares with some risk. The glaring fluorescent lights that burn all night inside the White Cross drugstore around it attract a swarm of Vegas's most desperate hard-luck cases: the homeless, the crack whores, the simply crazy and, not infrequently, the violent. Flitting in endlessly to pump away at the dozen or so quarter video poker machines near the rear door, they are continuously eyed by the bouncer-sized night clerk armed with mace, a billy club, and handcuffs.

My newfound moral smugness lasts only a few minutes; as I drive Oakey Street at about 5 A.M., my hands refuse to turn the steering wheel into the White Cross lot. Not out of fear certainly, as I eat there regularly. But, with respect to Dr. Hunter, it's out of compulsion that I continue gliding down Las Vegas Boulevard, slowly and easily cruising the Strip (now about the only time of day or night when it's free of gridlock). As if running on auto-pilot, I pass the gleaming Bellagio and make a right turn on Flamingo, go about a half-mile, and dock my car with the valet at the Palms casino.

Run by the Maloof family, which also owns the Sacramento Kings sports team, the Palms incarnates the Newest of the New Las Vegas. Home to the filming of a recent batch of the *Real World*—MTV's reality series starring sculpted but whining self-obsessers—the Palms, by comparison, makes the Hard Rock seem little more than the social hall at a Sun City retirement complex. Somehow evading antidiscriminatory hiring guidelines, the entire corps of the Palms' dealers, outfitted in ultra-hip uniforms of brightly colored, rayon bowling shirts, seems barely old enough to shave or menstruate. And unlike most any of the other casinos—which favor clean-cut wholesomeness—nose jewelry and tattoos seem *de rigueur* at the Palms. The canned rock music never dips below bone-shattering levels and rudely reverberates off the bleached hardwood floors. There's no let-up even at 5:15 in the morning. The parking beach teems with SUVs, gangsta rap and hip-hop banging through the darkened windows, hunks, babes, and hotties strutting their stuff in droves in this hour before dawn.

Catering to kids who don't know that the Brad Pitt version of *Ocean's Eleven* is a remake, the Palms' table games are among the worst in Vegas (though its "loose" machines are a locals' favorite). But I capitulate to my superstitions. There's one odd ten dollar minimum multi-deck, rip-off Blackjack table over near the roulette wheels, odd because it's low to the ground and accommodates average-height chairs instead of the usual raised stools, where, against all odds, I have had a couple of bountiful winning streaks. And to pile on the superstitions, it's always while I've been sitting at the last-to-play "third base" seat on the dealer's extreme right.

Pleased to find the table half-empty, I take my favorite seat, and cash in my surviving two hundred dollars worth of winnings for two stacks of reddish five-dollar chips. I see the dealer's shoe is midway through the six decks and I have no idea what cards have been played and what remains. But what difference does it make? To me this is a sucker's game not worth trying to track. I'm here betting on luck and I decide to play two hands simultaneously, placing four five-dollar chips on each spot (playing more than one hand requires a bet of at least twice the table minimum).

Rarely have I seen a dealer blaze at the hyper-speed pace set by the young Chinese woman running our table. As the fingertips of her left hand deftly pluck the cards from the clicking shoe, her right hand swings to the middle of the table, takes the cards from her left and snaps them down in place, while her left arcs back toward the repository of cards. Seen from the cameras above, her movements must seem like an accelerated and graceful dry-land breast stroke, her hair-covered face and upper torso bobbing to and fro as her arms sweep laterally across the table, establishing an undeniably erotic and transfixing rhythm.

While playing hand-dealt single-deck at a place like Binion's involves a skillful matching of wits with the cards, if not directly with the dealer, evoking a sense of ongoing, slightly upward struggle, the prevailing emotion at this multi-deck table is plain, cold, rushing fear. I feel as if bolted down and strapped into a careening, rocketing roller coaster, fighting to keep my eyes open and my thoughts clear, praying to not black out on the swooshing, twisting dives and fall-offs, hoping that soon I'll be back on the straight, uphill rise—before or avoiding one more precipitous dip. But unlike the ride at Space Mountain, there's no defined end to this cycle, unless you create it and bail out before getting sped off and whisked away again.

I don't have to make that decision. No need to bail. The Palms' multi-deck Blackjack table abruptly spits me out and dumps me less than five minutes after I sat down. I think I won one hand, maybe two out of maybe fifteen or twenty. Otherwise, the encounter was as unilateral, as laughingly one-sided, as the American invasion of Iraq. Except no one's laughing. When my last chip is gone, there are no condolences from the dealer or the two drunken kids from Long Island playing to my right, no respectful dimming of the lights, no interruption of the rock muzak for a public service announcement, no thank you from the Maloofs. Only the briefest pause, really just a minor hesitation from the dealer, her gaze gently querying me as our eyes temporarily lock, waiting to see if I make some gesture suggesting I will pull out more cash from my pants. In the same split-second I ponder the same question but, nevertheless, stand up and walk away. Before I can rise she's already back to frenetically stroking the cards.

On the short drive back downtown I hear on the radio that the U.S. troops that have entered Baghdad intend to stay. I wonder how long they will be there. I also wonder when will be the next time I play cards. For now, all I want to do is get back to Binion's, get to my room, get some sleep, and dream about neither Iraq nor Blackjack.

Paradise and Perdition:
Betting on Benny

SINCE THE DEATH OF the Desert Inn, I have retreated a couple miles north into Las Vegas's old and slowly decaying downtown, specifically to its most notorious and most historically colorful property, Binion's Horseshoe. This is where I now camp.

While Las Vegas's international image today is banked on the shimmering Strip, that stretch of world-famous mega-resorts in fact prospers beyond the city limits and is part of greater, unincorporated Clark County. As the mob opened the first resorts on the mostly barren Strip of the late '40s and early '50s, just south of Las Vegas proper, they asked the city to link them up to its sewer system. The small city, not wanting to spend money on added infrastructure, refused. Out of need, Bugsy Siegel's Flamingo, the El Rancho Vegas, and the gangster-operated Thunderbird resorts put together their own sanitation district and in 1953 the unincorporated patch took on the official name of Paradise. At one point the city tried to annex the growing Strip, but, by a 90 percent margin, the county residents voted against the idea. By then it became obvious to the Strip's operators that it was in their economic and political interest to stay outside the city limits, thereby eluding taxes and any bothersome political meddling.

Talk about a losing bet. Las Vegas City Hall, today dwarfed by the walloping political power exercised by the surrounding Clark County and the economic clout of its Casino Row, can only deeply regret the historic error committed by never absorbing the gold-paved strip of highway to its immediate south when it could. All it had to do was hook up the sewer lines. That never-completed connection means that today not a penny in Strip gambling or property taxes makes its way into the city's perennially strapped treasury. The current city of Las Vegas proper comprises barely a third of the county's 1.5 million population, and its decaying downtown inner core struggles for attention and survival while the shimmering Strip captures global fascination. Ninety-six percent of the Strip and two hundred thousand residents flourish right outside the Las Vegas city limits in its self-made Paradise, the most heavily-populated unincorporated non-city in America.

There was a time when downtown's central Fremont Street was the pulsating main artery of Las Vegas, the first street in the city to be paved and the first, in 1956, to grow a high-rise. After miles of neon tubing in the 1940s were draped along its hotels and gambling halls, and the brightly lit waving Cowboy Vic was erected in 1947, Fremont Street morphed into Glitter Gulch—an illuminated urban canyon of casinos memorialized in millions of postcards and still photos. This, not the then-embryonic Strip, was the original graphic mental image held by millions when they thought of Las Vegas. Fremont Street was also its main visitor draw. It *was* Las Vegas. With the smaller, mostly family-owned downtown casinos—including the Horseshoe—butted one up against each other, Fremont Street became a rare exceptional zone of American public permissiveness—much like New Orleans' Bourbon Street—where tourists and gamblers could carouse all night, drinks in hand, hopping or staggering from one gambling table to another while police did little to interfere other than to referee the chaos. The casual, if not outright proletarian or cowboy atmosphere, the cheap eats, penny slots, and the low table minimums made downtown that much more attractive to millions.

With the unprecedented boom of the Strip in the '60s and '70s, and certainly by the time of its pyramid-pirate-and-volcano Disneyfication in the early '90s, downtown's older, more traditional casinos started plummeting into decline, consistently losing more and more revenue to their corporate mega-competitors. Last year the Strip casinos stacked up $4.7 billion in gambling revenues while only $657 million was wagered downtown.

The same man, Steve Wynn, who generated so much of the suffocating economic pressure on downtown also helped to partially revive it—in part because of his own investment in the old Golden Nugget casino, just off of Fremont. In 1995, under Wynn's leadership, the major downtown casinos inaugurated the seventy-million-dollar Fremont Street Experience, turning four blocks of the historic street into an air-conditioned pedestrian mall covered by a ninety-foot-high space-age canopy. Studded with literally millions of lightbulbs and hundreds of speakers powered by 540,000 watts of audio, 6 times nightly the canopy becomes a mammoth-sized overhead projection screen for a free, 10-minute light-and-sound show.

This one-of-a-kind spectacle competes strongly with any other "attraction" down south on the Strip, drawing thousands of awe-struck and applauding visitors who crane their heads upward to soak in each show. But, as noted, even with another one hundred million dollars or so in recent additions and expansions of the original Fremont experience, downtown's resuscitation is only partial, and its prognosis unsure. Some downtown operators have conjured rather exotic remedies for their predicament. The Boyd family, which runs the aging California, Fremont, and much snazzier Main Street Station casinos, all within steps of each other on the edge of downtown, has maintained a direct pipeline with Hawaiian tourists. Running its own islands-based Vacations-Hawaii travel agency, Boyd as much as funnels tens of thousands of Hawaiian customers each year directly through the doors of its downtown casinos, which reciprocate with a mostly Asian staff, various "Aloha" specials, and Pacific Rim cuisine.

But leave the mall-like canopy on Fremont Street, cross Las Vegas Boulevard, and you immediately descend into a world much more striking than a transplanted piece of Honolulu. The canopy, in fact, serves also as a sort of funnel: pour out of its east end and come face to face with the threadbare remnants of the original city. If the Strip is Paradise, this must be Purgatory, if not outright Perdition. Among its twenty-five-dollars-a-throw hot-sheet motels, round-the-clock pawn shops, bail bondsmen, tattoo parlors, check-cashing joints, liquor stores, and even vampire-like blood banks, moves and wanders much of the city's permanent army of derelicts, homeless and busted out. Zigzagging among them, you half expect to bump into a reeking, collapsing Nick Cage on his way out from *Leaving Las Vegas*. Inside Fremont Street's vintage El Cortez Hotel, so antiquated that its marquis still announces nonexistent "floor shows," a sign near its elevator says that hotel security personnel are available to escort patrons to the parking lot.

Among this surreal mix of downtown multimillion-dollar casinos and flea-bag hotels, among the Japanese tourists, the coupon clippers, the professional gamblers, and needle-jamming junkies, there are no scale models of the Eiffel Tower or Lady Liberty, nor any stucco-and-plaster reproductions of the Roman Forum. Instead, on the corner of Second Street and Ogden, a few steps from Fremont across from the casino that bears his name, marooned on a string of parking beaches, protected by a waist-high iron fence, yet thoroughly ignored by the thousands of daily passers-by, stands the flood-lit statue of Benny Binion on horse-back—about the only monument to a real human anywhere in Vegas. In a classic cowboy suit, a ten gallon hat, and mounted on the sort of steed he used to rustle as a youth, Binion's bronze likeness bears little resemblance, say, to the Che Guevara statue that once stood in Santiago or the monuments to Augusto Sandino in Managua. To think of him in any sense as a revolutionary or humanitarian is beyond absurdity. But in modern Las Vegas, Benny Binion, who died on Christmas Day in 1989, is as close as you're possibly going to get to an Everyman's anticorporate icon. And his surviving family's hotel and casino, in which I'm bunkered on the third floor, feels much like the last bastion of stubborn, dogged resistance to the packaged, filed-down, pre-digested "entertainment experience" pushed by the competing big operators and their Ivy-League strategists and accountants. This notion, too, is an overly romantic extrapolation, but in a city where expectations are calculated down to the nth degree, you take whatever wrinkles history provides.

"A barbaric outlaw of terrifying means," a racketeer, bootlegger, and cold killer is how Binion is correctly described by Denton and Morris in *The Money and the Power*. Even the official Binion Horseshoe company web site today boasts that before its founder moved from Texas to Vegas in 1946 he would pack "three pistols—two .45 automatics and a small .38 revolver" and it characterizes his 1931 fatal shooting of a rival "fellow bootlegger" as an act of "athletic marksmanship." (In his later years, Binion downgraded to a single .45 Colt Commander and eventually to a puny .22 magnum, according to journalist A.D. Hopkins). But Binion was also a prescient casino entrepreneur, known for running the most honest game in Vegas, of taking any bet no matter how big, including the legendary $777,000 single wager that William Lee Bergstrom laid down in 1980 on a dice table "Don't Pass" line—and won. "Binion's legacy," says historian Mike Green, "is that he invented what you might call the downtown approach. His attitude was, you treat a millionaire and a guy who has holes in his pockets the same way—like a millionaire. Of course, millionaires get treated a bit better. But it means that the Horseshoe is open and welcoming to all comers."

Born north of Dallas in 1904, Binion went to work at age ten and soon took over his household from a father who was a drunk and a gambler. Moving from smuggling to horse rustling, high jacking, and bootlegging, Binion worked his way up the hierarchy of the local Dallas mob. By the early 1940s he was knee-deep in money and illegal casinos and received a personal visit from Meyer Lansky, who came to Texas to personally check out a colorful character, and possible future business partner, that he had heard so much about.

When a national gang war spilled over into Dallas in 1946, and Binion found himself on the losing side, the official legend is that he packed his five kids and several suitcases of cash into a chauffer-driven Cadillac, and like so many hustlers of his era, headed right for Vegas. Binion bought right into the downtown casino scene. And in August 1951, with assistance from his old acquaintance Meyer Lansky, he opened Benny Binion's Horseshoe Club.

From the outset, Binion catered to his clients and would gladhand and backslap them when they came to visit him where he could usually be found, in the front booth of the casino coffee shop. He more or less invented the notion of "comping" the gamblers, he was the first to offer free drinks, and his casino was the first downtown place to lay down carpets. Barely literate, he was unparalleled in reading people—and their needs. "If you want to get rich, make little people feel big . . . good food cheap, good whiskey cheap and a good gamble. That's all there is to it, son," is how Hopkins quotes Binion's "gnomic wisdom." Once asked to compare his Horseshoe with the glitzier Strip competitors, Binion said: "We got a little joint and a big bankroll, and all them others got a big joint and no bankroll."

Binion temporarily lost control of the casino when he did a stretch of prison time for felony tax evasion, dating back to his Texas days. But when he came back to operate the Horseshoe, he imprinted on it an image of the most straightforward, no-pretense haven for what one local academic calls "stone cold gambling." A seven-foot-high gold horseshoe, placed near the door, it's see-through arch packed with a million dollars worth of ten-thousand-dollar bills, was the lay totem whose spirit ruled the house and inspired the acolytes.

By the time of his death, rather appropriately at almost the same moment the New Vegas was birthed with the opening of the Mirage, Benny Binion was a key player in Nevada politics and didn't blush much if asked about having bribed—or attempted to bribe—a long list of commissioners, congressmen, and senators. His casino was also known to have a darker side. In the mob days, extra-legal street justice was commonly practiced in numerous Vegas gambling houses. At Binion's, it persisted beyond its own era. Binion's hired thugs and casino henchmen were still beating up cheats, room burglars, and petty thieves and throwing them into alley dumpsters well into the 1970s. In 1979 an angry customer, coming off a losing streak, complained that the house had cheated him. Rushed out of the casino, he was shot point-blank in the head with a gun that was later found in the casino vault. No witnesses would testify and no charges were ever pressed. Accusations and lawsuits over players getting roughed up still flickered for years to come as Benny's children took over management and in 1985, the Binions paid out a $675,000 settlement to two aggrieved customers.

It's safe to say those days are now over and the greatest peril present at Binion's today is the potential for frittering away your paycheck. But that tradition of little-guy democratic materialism imposed by its founder still prevails inside the Horseshoe casino. Sitting next to you at the Blackjack table, or crowding your elbows at the craps table is just as likely to be a frugal Midwestern auntie taking advantage of the low minimums or a boisterous Oklahoma oil man pitching stacks of gray-and-pink five-hundred-dollar chips, or a grizzled and committed Blackjack strategist trying to ace the tables.

No bountiful buffet is offered (except during the annual World Series of Poker which Binion craftily concocted in 1970), there's no lounge, no showroom, and no live entertainment— except for the unfailingly diverse cast of players and veteran dealers. Blue-collar snack bars serve up bowls of chili and mountainous corned-beef sandwiches. The fading hotel rooms are from the low-end stock of a Holiday Inn. There's no extravagant hotel lobby, merely a registration desk—seemingly lifted from a Motel 8—adjacent to the poker room.

The dark, low-ceilinged, dimly lit playing floor, with its New Orleans–style polished mahogany and brass, covered in bordello-red velvet wallpaper, its card tables pushed close to each other, many of its dealers wizened pros who first hit town in the '50s or even the late '40s, has much more the feel of a gambling saloon than a gaming casino. The four rows of Blackjack tables, with only a couple of exceptions, give the player unadulterated, unshaved, hand-dealt single-deck—the best, most advantageous game in town. The crowded craps tables give some of the highest-paying odds in the city and are run by croupiers still allowed to hustle the games in a time-honored tradition that has been snuffed out in the corporate casinos. Binion's embodies an era and ethic that overlaps and even predates the Rat Pack Cool of the demolished Desert Inn. If the Strip resorts and casinos are, as they promise, "adult playgrounds," then the Horseshoe is just plain for adults. I don't go to Binion's to play. I go to Binion's to gamble. If Vegas is the Major Leagues of gambling, then Binion's is its Fenway Park.

"Binion's is a living museum, a gambler's museum," says Bill Friedman, a former casino manager and the author of the industry bible on casino design. "If it goes, it's going to be a great and terrible loss." Like the rest of its downtown neighbors, Binion's—which relies heavily on visitors who drive in rather than fly to Vegas—has been battered by the rapid-fire opening of palatial Indian casinos throughout California.

"Downtown is at best just holding on," says UNLV's Bill Thompson. "It's dependent on a drive-in trade that love slot machines, and those people will no longer drive the extra time to get here when they can find an Indian casino two or three hours closer to their homes." In February 2003, the *Las Vegas Review-Journal* reported that Binion's has been "bleeding red ink" and that its current owner, Becky Binion Behnen "has been forced to plow millions in personal funds to keep the failing property open." The casino was also behind in its payments to employee pension funds, had slashed workers' medical benefits, and was about $2.5 million in arrears for its contributions to the cooperative Fremont Street Experience and its lighted canopy.

A few months before, one day in the fall of 2002, I was stupefied to walk into Binion's and find hundreds of its slot machines shut down and roped off with yellow tape, along with several of its gaming tables. State gaming regulators had ordered the partial shutdown because the casino's on-hand cash had fallen below the required level to cover the amounts wagered by players. (Casinos are mandated to hold enough real money in their cages to simultaneously pay off all of the chips in play.) Within a few days, Binion's coffers were restocked and the gaming areas reopened but it was an ominous episode, a long way to come from the salad days when Benny Binion, rumored to have suitcases of cash in his basement, was downtown's unofficial short-term lender and would gladly come up with a million bucks or so for the neighboring and rival casinos when they would find themselves scraping bottom.

Binion's troubles are little mystery. The Horseshoe now suffers from the same squeeze that any ma-and-pa market does trying to survive when the corporate big boxes pop open across the street. Management by Benny's heirs has also proved turbulent, even lurid, and that disorder has reverberated into the family business. After his death, his children, Jack, Ted, Brenda, and Becky, ran the place in a clannish, tribal mode, lugubriously making consensual decisions on the most minor of details. Ted had apparently inherited his father's stallion soul and brought much of his freewheeling spirit into the casino. Jack Binion was the more serious businessman and concentrated much of his energy on extending the Binion's franchise into new legalized gambling venues in Louisiana and Mississippi.

Ted, meanwhile, wrestled with a long-time drug addiction, known as "chasin' the dragon," heating up black-tar heroin and inhaling the smoke. Ted also had a penchant for hanging out with gangsters and gunmen and in the late 1980s he had his gaming license suspended. After submitting to regular drug tests, Ted's license was restored but his hard living down-spiraled toward disaster.

A 1995 excursion to the Cheetah's girlie club introduced Ted to comely twenty-three-year-old California dancer Sandra Murphy. After losing thirteen thousand dollars at the Caesar's Palace Blackjack tables, Murphy was more than ready to pal up with the casino heir whose estimated seventy-five-million-dollar personal fortune helped buy her a new Mercedes and high-publicity Neiman Marcus shopping sprees. Ted's continued public association with mobsters, in this case with reputed Chicago gangster Herbie Blitzstein, led the state to definitively terminate his gaming license and place him on the list of "Excluded Persons," barring him forever from every Nevada casino, including that of his own family.

Forced to remove his personal belongings from the Horseshoe vaults, Ted Binion asked a newly made acquaintance, Rick Tabish, to organize the relocation of his stash of forty-six thousand pounds of silver bars, worth about seven million dollars. Tabish and his crew, with a shot-gun armed Ted Binion at his side, reburied the pirate's booty in a specially made underground vault in the middle of the dusty town of Pahrump, seventy miles north of Las Vegas.

A few months later, on September 17, 1998, Ted's girlfriend Sandy Murphy made a 911 call and had paramedics dispatched to Binion's Vegas home. Ted Binion was sprawled out dead on his living-room floor, an empty bottle of antidepressants and partially spent doses of heroin at his side. His reputed gangster buddy Herbie Blitzstein had been bumped off a few months before and initial suspicions linked the two murders.

That is until two days later, when Rick Tabish, the friend who had helped him hide his secret treasure, and two other men were caught red-handed as they were trying to dig up Ted's twenty-three tons of silver. Subsequent investigations and the ensuing trial and conviction of Tabish and Sandy Murphy revealed they were lovers who conspired in the murder-robbery. Tabish apparently had pulled a gun on Ted Binion, handcuffed him, and poured more than a hundred Xanax tablets and nearly a half liter of tar heroin down his throat. As a final indignity, Binion was forced to watch Tabish and Murphy have sex in front of him before he was suffocated.

Just months before the murder, Ted's sister, Becky, finally succeeded into forcing her siblings to sell her of all their interests in the Horeshoe. She had argued that her brother Jack was too preoccupied with his Mississippi operation and that the Vegas Horseshoe was in neglect.

Becky claimed to be restoring her father's style in taking over the casino, repeatedly citing "daddy" to a visiting reporter. But to many industry observers, her management of the Horseshoe—aided by husband Nick Behnen and their son Benny Jr.—has been rather lackluster, penny-wise and dollar-foolish. Credit and comp policies have been tightened, the historic high-wager limits have been lowered, and sometimes even two-hundred-dollar Blackjack bettors find excessive "heat"—pit surveillance and supervision—applied to their tables. In 1999 Becky Behnen stunned casino regulars and loyalists when she sold off her dad's prized million-dollar golden horseshoe for a rumored profit of four million dollars, what many think was only a shortsighted move. "A big, big mistake," says gambling author Max Rubin. "Standing next to the horseshoe and the million bucks was the free picture everyone coming to downtown would take. Where else could the average guy get that close to a million? Benny, like few others, deeply understood how much the casino atmosphere matters."

Late at night, Horseshoe Blackjack pit man Kenny Franks, now with forty-six years in the business, having worked in almost two dozen gambling houses, takes me to the window of the Horseshoe gift shop on the near-deserted mezzanine level. "Unbelievable how many of these guys I can remember," he says, nodding toward a large sepia-toned, wood-framed photograph on the other side of the glass. It's a group shot of three dozen or so of the participants in the first-ever World Series of Poker in 1970, a tournament that this year drew more than eight hundred contestants to Binion's. Benny Binion, aged and grizzled, appears in the middle foreground, one of his arms draped around fellow Texan and actor Chill Wills. Kenny's index finger slides across the glass and he ticks off the names as if this were his high school graduation picture. "They're all dead now," he says. "But that there's Jimmy Casella, a shylock who had like five million dollars on the street. Joe Bernstein, he was a professional gambler . . . Titantic Thompson, now that guy was the best card pitcher in the world . . . Wild Bill Free ran naked through the Dunes one night yelling 'Top this, motherfucker!' . . . Don Lee? He was a champion card-mucker. He knew how to jiggle the handle of slot machines to make them pay off. Don helped me run the Jolly Trolley casino for the New Jersey guys . . . Natie Blank over there on the end, an alleged killer and shylock who always wore an alpaca sweater . . . Jack Strauss . . . he won one of these poker tournaments after being down to his last chip . . . and that guy there is old Johnny Luke. He was said to be the owner of the real best little whorehouse in Texas."

Kenny spends another ten minutes or so in reverie, trying to place the other faces to thousands of names he's collected over the decades that he still cuts and stacks in his head like so many playing chips. As I quietly stare deeper into this ghostly picture, it's brownish monochromatic tone making it appear a half-century older than it is, I'm certain that it inadvertently froze the final, closing moments of a particular chapter in American and Las Vegas history. What I'm not certain is if I'm peering only into the Horseshoe's past, or also into its encroaching future.

G-String Politics:
A Neon Tijuana

THE DAM HOLDING BACK the full fury of the brimming
dance-club scandal has finally burst wide open and,
overnight, all Las Vegas is awash in a neck-deep who's-
buying-who corruption story that rivals the best of pulp fiction,
blows the clothes off the ethos, as it is, of Southern Nevada politics, and swamps the careers of several leading politicians.

In a probe that both intersects and surpasses the crackdown
earlier in the year on Rick Rizzolo's Crazy Horse Too, in an
encore performance, dozens of assault rifle–toting FBI agents
just swarmed two other Vegas lap-dance clubs—Jaguars and
Cheetahs—owned by the local Galardi family. The family's
clubs in San Diego were also raided. Cheetahs, of course, was
also once the employer of Sandy Murphy, the young dancer convicted of bumping off Teddy Binion.

The federal agents storming the Vegas properties came with

warrants seeking "all campaign contribution records from 1997 made on behalf or by" the two boob-bars, as well as all "records including ledgers or journals or handwritten notes of payments or gifts" to a passel of high-profile local pols.

Caught up in the new federal probe is Rizzolo's old friend, former cop and current city councilman Mike McDonald, the powerful chairwoman of the county commission Mary Kincaid-Chauncey and her hubby (also an ex-cop), and two other former county commissioners who have also been candidates for higher office, Erin Kenney and Dario Herrera along with his wife Emily. All are suspected of taking bribes and payoffs from the Galardi family and their club operations in exchange for political favors. Even juicier, Lance Malone, the suspected go-between and bag man, a paid "consultant" to the Galardis, is himself an ex-county commissioner *and* an ex-cop *and* an ex-Mormon who at times has railed against the immorality of the dance-club spectacle.

Does this get any better?

Yes.

As the scandal unfolds, Councilman McDonald—a conservative locked in a re-election battle for his political life—now publicly admits he's also a salaried "consultant" to the Galardis, though he won't say since when or for how much. "I used my knowledge, not my influence," he pleads rather lamely.

Then another incumbent City Councilman, Michael Mack, who apparently is not a subject of this probe, nevertheless finds out that among the club surveillance video tape seized by the FBI from Cheetah's is footage of him getting a racy lap-dance from a writhing young gal. The twice-divorced, currently-engaged conservative who has built a pawn-shop empire and already survived a couple of other ethical jams, figures he'd better cut his losses and he now announces that he, too, is a paid consultant to a strip club. But breathe easy and get out your scorecards, because Mack claims that now he's not only abstaining from such lewd activity but that, anyways, he's not in the employ of the tainted and scrutinized Galardis. His contract binds him, instead, to the upstanding Eiliades family that owns several other dance clubs and that is scheduled to open the luxurious titty cabaret *Treasures,* a few months from now. Though not all observers appreciated his belated candor nor his argument that he was generously providing information the public release of which really ought to be left to the discretion of his clients. ("Huh?" editorialized a bemused *Las Vegas Sun.* "Earth to Mr. Mack: If somebody providing an elected official with outside income doesn't like the fact that his name may end up on a disclosure form, he should do business elsewhere.")

Well said. But the local press also ought to be asking itself some equally tough questions. Like, how is it that two city councilmen—one who's locked in a tight re-election campaign—and a former county commissioner can be on the payrolls of sleazy club operators and it takes the Feds to find out?

All of which speaks to the bigger issue of Nevada and, specifically, Vegas politics. Dominated by the sin industries, no local politician has ever paid a price for taking money from either the gambling or dance-club interests—much the same way few eyebrows are raised by Iowa politicians in the thrall of the farm lobbies or California pols befriended by the movie studios.

Taking campaign contributions from dominant local industry is, unfortunately, American politics and business-as-usual. That's not supposed to include, however, under-the-table bribes, naked influence-buying, and egregious conflict-of-interest consulting contracts.

This scandal also bares the pointlessness of trying to identify Nevada politicians solely or even primarily by their professed ideology. Maybe because the role of money, in every sense, is so much more straightforward here, there are few places in the country where party identification means so very little.

Ponder some of this state's apparent philosophical contradictions: It's a right-to-work state but with one of the highest union densities in the country. It's branded with a strong libertarian imprimatur tolerating gambling and prostitution yet its voters turned down gay marriage and marijuana decriminalization measures. Democrats and Republicans evenly divvy up its congressional delegation. It's Republican Governor is battling brutally with anti-tax conservatives in his own party. And the corporate casino industry, about the only business paying visible taxes in a no–income tax state, often joins with liberal Democrats in wanting to tax *other* industries.

The burgeoning dance-club scandal reveals the political fault lines in Las Vegas as something even more sordid than the usual Republican/Democrat partisan divide. Instead, the whole affair is reminiscent—albeit without the accompanying bloodshed—of the tragicomic wars last decade that shook Tijuana and most of surrounding Baja California. Different factions of the local Mexican government went on the pad of competing drug lords and it all culminated in a horrific and deadly urban shoot-out between the investigative police of Baja California, and the investigative police of the Mexican federal government, each agency fronting for rival drug cartels.

In Vegas, there's been no shooting. But the implicated politicians have apparently been doing their dirty work as soldiers in the no-prisoners economic war raging among the different club-owning families. And the Galardis, it seems, have even switched their largess from one political rival to another when it has benefited their business.

Liberals, even progressives, should refrain from gloating that councilmen/consultants McDonald and Mack, as well as Galardi bag-man Malone, are conservatives. In Las Vegas politics, money trumps all ideological posturing. Former county commissioner Herrera was once touted as a promising Democratic hope for Congress by the left-of-center *American Prospect* (he lost the 2002 race, scoring a paltry 19 percent of the vote). In 2002, a federal general inspector opened a probe of contracting at the Las Vegas Housing Authority after news reports revealed that Herrera, while serving on the elected County Commission, also held— yes—a forty-two-thousand-dollar consulting contract with the Authority, whose board members said they knew nothing of the arrangement.

Fellow Democrat Erin Kinney, who gave up her county commission seat to make an unsuccessful run for lieutenant governor, has consistently garnered substantial labor union support.

And County Commission Chair Mary Kincaid-Chauncey, often described as a compassionate and gentle grandmotherly type who runs Kincaid's Flower Korner and who has taken in a flock of foster children, has reportedly been captured on FBI wiretaps accepting an envelope stuffed with five thousand dollars in cash from Galardi delivery boy, Lance Malone. News reports say she later opened the envelope, saw the cash, and confirmed that she received it when Malone later contacted her. She claims she then innocently deposited the money in a "trust-fund" account set up to support a relative's athletic program for disadvantaged kids.

Whatever Kincaid-Chauncey's explanations about the cash payoff, neither she or anyone else will have an easy time explaining away a couple of 1999 county commission decisions that were so bizarre, so directly cadged from the Tijuana drug-wars playbook that they ignited the federal probe that has been quietly simmering for the past few years.

In early 1999 the Galardis were worried that their Cheetah's club and their planned Jaguars would be threatened by the proposed opening of a competing cabaret nearby. Then-County Commissioner Lance Malone, publicly inveighing against the spread of Demon Vice, pushed an ordinance to block new dance clubs. Mike McDonald came over from the city council and also pitched the county commission on behalf of Malone. Erin Kinney joined in the move together with Malone to make the ordinance retroactive so that, in effect, Galardi's new club could open but his competitor would be blocked.

A court ruling quickly overturned the commission's blatantly unfair regulation. But another commission vote in the same period was no less than a gold-plated favor for the club-owning family, a glaring and toadying political favor that in almost any other venue would have raised a chorus-call for mass impeachments.

As Maio Galardi proceeded to open his ritzy Jaguars club, local licensing officials had some serious concerns. As part of a standard background investigation before they gave a nod to Jaguars, they wanted to know what exactly the connection was between Mario Galardi's father and business partner Jack Galardi and the infamous Gold Card cabaret in Atlanta, the target of a well-publicized federal grand jury and reputedly run as part of an organized crime syndicate. (The Vegas Jaguars club originally was also to be called the Gold Card).

Metro police officials came before the county commission in the summer of 1999 and asked for twenty-four thousand dollars to fund the background investigation of the Galardis, including sending some detectives to Atlanta. The funds, by the way, would have to come from the Galardis, whose estimated worth at the time was more than twenty-five million dollars. Yet, Commissioner Malone—a supposed vocal conservative critic of public degeneracy—publicly complained that the amount requested was "a lot of money for any business" to have to spend. The police then offered a more limited investigation at less than half the price. But a majority of conservative Commissioner Lance Malone, and the more liberal Dario Herrera and Erin Kenny, along with a fourth member of the county governing board, said at the decisive meeting that it would be unfair to further delay Galardi's new club merely because of a grand jury investigation about which he claimed to know nothing. The four-to-three vote immediately cleared the way for Jaguars, though the same commission had recently bent over backward to block a competitor. In the free-for-all political atmosphere of Las Vegas, there was little public outcry, let alone outrage, over the way the commission snuggled and spooned with the Galardis. But the Joint Federal Organized Crime Task Force based in the city could hardly believe what it was seeing and began its own investigation. The rest is history—or, at least, history in the making. The politicians voting to protect Galardi were apparently taking direct bribes from him.

Andrea Hackett, of the Las Vegas Dancers Alliance, still looking for work, has been zealously tracking the dance-club scandal. Worried that it will create a backlash that might impact the future of local adult entertainment, she sees at least one benefit coming from the political debacle. "This might be it when it comes to the political clout of the clubs," she says. "What politician is going to want to get within a hundred yards now of a strip club owner? This might be good for us," she says of her intentions to continue organizing the dancers. "The clubs might be losing their political allies."

The political toll is already mounting. A few weeks after the scandal breaks, Mike McDonald loses his close city council reelection race to newcomer Janet Moncrief, a true political nobody.

This only adds to the glee of the guy who can most gloat over the unfolding scandal: Las Vegas's highest-volume full-time gadfly, the wealthy and conservative Republican Steve Miller, who served on the city council between 1987 and 1991. Having made a fortune off the Vegas souvenir business and the ubiquitous dice-encrusted clock that he patented, Miller freely spends most of his time being a pain-in-the-ass to local politicians. His *American-mafia.com* web site, to which he devotes Herculean energy, regularly and stridently denounces what he sees as, well, the new incarnation of the Vegas mob, and has endlessly battered away at the nexus of girlie clubs and local politics.

This is definitely his I-Told-You-So moment.

A fierce critic of Mayor Goodman, former Councilman McDonald (who used to be his friend, as did Lance Malone), and of all of the pols implicated in the breaking scandal, as well as of Rick Rizzolo and other dance-club owners, Miller himself has, at one time or another, been a front-line material witness to much of Vegas's political incest—or make that a participant.

Tracking his moves are like trying to freeze-frame a dropping roulette ball. In one of his many political campaigns, Miller ran against his former friend McDonald in the 2003 primary. After losing, he supported challenger Moncrief. But just days after Moncrief was sworn in, Miller accused her of selling out to tainted club interests and told the press that he had "conspired" with her to break Nevada political campaign laws, zig-zags that seem to perfectly reflect his erratic positions.

When I meet with the tall, thin fifty-eight year old at his spacious home near the Palace Station casino, Miller derides a city government that allows teenage girls to dance totally nude but then is quick to disclose that he's the landlord of the always-packed topless Paradise Club, across the street from the Hard Rock Hotel and Casino. "But I just own the dirt," he says. "I've owned the lot for decades, not the club" which he goes on at length to describe as only the classiest and most wholesome sort of venue.

And while he expresses disgust with the news of the alleged pay-offs of politicians, he tells me about the campaign contributions that he accepted, on more than one occasion, from none other than the Galardis. "But those were legal, political contributions, not under-the-table cash," he says. "There's a big difference between a political contribution and a cash pay-off."

That's not just a defensive hedge by Miller. That's his entire, aggressively argued point. Indeed, maybe no one better than Miller embodies the professed public ethic of Vegas politics. The problem isn't the clubs, or their political influence, or the relationships they maintain with political power—so long as it is all legal and in the open. Period. Otherwise, he's shocked—just shocked to find out things have gone too far. But the stories he tells of club owners playing one politician off against another are mind-boggling.

Originally, Miller says, he knew Mario Galardi only as a "fellow Republican."

"I knew him," he says, "as the guy who would use his mansion, just a couple of blocks from here, for all the ultra-conservative, right-to-life, right-wing fundraisers. That's where I'd see him all the time. And I'd think, 'This is just amazing.'"

But when he tried to unseat then-Mayor Jan Jones in the 1991 elections, Miller found Galardi seeking him out. He explains that, at the time, it was the Galardis who were the underdog upstarts in the dance-club rivalries. The more powerful Rick Rizzolo of the Crazy Horse Too was using his political assets, namely Councilman Mike McDonald, to put a crimp on the Galardis. "Galardi was so upset that he gave me a five-thousand-dollar contribution, hoping I could get in and head off the pressure from McDonald."

Miller lost the mayor's race. But he took political contributions from Galardi again in 1994 when he failed in his bid for lieutenant governor, and again in 1995 when he tried and failed to unseat McDonald from the city council. "Galardi gave me that contribution because he clearly wanted me to take out McDonald who was harassing him," Miller says with a smile. "But when I lost, Galardi solved his problem by putting McDonald on his payroll. That was his foothold in the city. But he also needed clout in the county. That's when he hired [ex-commissioner] Lance Malone."

Miller proudly boasts that one legal political contribution he did turn down during one of his quixotic and failed campaigns was from Crazy Horse Too operator Rick Rizzolo. "I couldn't move quick enough to send that check back in the mail," he says proudly. That anecdote leaves me somewhat perplexed, stumped to figure out what the moral difference is between a Rizzolo and a Galardi contribution, if any. I'm also thrown off by Miller's insistence that it's this year's earlier raid of Rizzolo's Crazy Horse Too and not the current probe of the Galardi operation that is the more politically significant of the two. That contradicts all available evidence, the assessment of just about every other serious political observer, not to speak of common sense.

A paranoid suspicion creeps up on me. In speaking to Miller, might I be entrapped in some weird warp of Vegas's *Matrix*-like politics wherein one set of tainted club owners are championed over their rivals? I don't think so. Miller's reputation is that he's weird and self-promoting, but honest. But, then again, who knows?

A personal parable he recounts to me with great gusto leaves me further wondering about just where the line of impropriety gets drawn through Vegas politics. Miller recalls a lunch on the Strip one day some years ago with Vegas's former and not-so-straight Sheriff Ralph Lamb, a top cop who was known to take sizeable so-called "loans" from Benny Binion. "Ralph and I are sitting and eating and I'll never forget the way he moved his finger on the table," Miller says, making the gliding, graceful motion of an experienced dealer sliding chips across the smooth, green-felt surface. "There he is moving that hand on the table and he says to me: 'In the old days it was two for you and one for me. Later it became two for me and one for you. And when no one said boo about that it just became three for me and fuck you.' "

I'm not sure what Miller's precise point is. But he does make a final prediction that I know is dead wrong. When I ask if the scandal is going to spread to Mayor Goodman's office, Miller jumps to say, "Oh yes, yes. Oscar's the main man. He's so deep into this he'll never get out."

That seems like the worst bet in town.

Mayor Big O:
"Nobody Tells on You"

T HE CURRENT POLITICAL CORRUPTION scandal is to sixty-three-year-old Las Vegas mayor Oscar Goodman what light showers might have meant to Noah. Don't even bother with an umbrella.

Once the lawyer-of-choice to America's most powerful and often most notorious gangsters, including Meyer Lansky, a history—by the way—that he openly celebrates rather than denies, what could Mayor Goodman possibly care about his own long-standing connections to some of the embroiled dance-club owners? This is the guy, after all, who played himself in a role in Scorsese's 1995 Vegas underworld saga, *Casino*.

Here's a boundlessly popular, multimillionaire mayor who once said he'd rather have a daughter date his old and deceased gangster client Tony Spilotro than an FBI agent; who often meets with constituents in bars and taverns in gatherings called "Martinis

With the Mayor"; who called Bush Administration energy secretary Spencer Abraham "that piece of garbage" for recommending that nearby Yucca Mountain be used as a nuclear waste dump; who said he'd like to "whack" the publisher of the biggest local paper; and who invited lap dancers to come into his city limits and grind away however they damn well pleased after the county commission restricted their movements last year.

The outside press says he's called "The Big O." But I've never heard anyone in Vegas call him that. The mayor's just known as Oscar. Plain old Oscar, as if Vegas was just down the road from Mayberry. And every time the mayor shoots his mouth off, his popularity ratings ratchet up another notch. With good reason he's on a first-name basis with the citizenry. Reelected earlier this year for a second four-year term, Goodman racked up a towering 87 percent of the vote, without doubt making him the most popular mayor in America.

Goodman, then, can hardly be losing any sleep over the current dance-club scandal when it was he who recently invited his former client and convicted felon Joey Cusamano to his daughter's engagement party. When asked by the press why he would host alleged mobster Cusamano, who appears in the Black Book of undesirables banned from all Nevada casinos, the mayor unapologetically replied: "What I do in my home is nobody's business."

Rick Rizzolo, the controversial and scrutinized owner of the Crazy Horse Too, has also been one of Goodman's clients and one of his campaign contributors. So what, Goodman has said, "My old clients used to pay me with bags of cash." At least Rizzolo handed him a check that had to be reported.

That's pretty much the same unflinching response I get when I finally meet up with the mayor. On a steamy weekday afternoon,

I find him sitting behind his tarmac-sized desk on the top, tenth floor of City Hall, behind his left shoulder a tray full of bluish bottles of Bombay Sapphire Gin—a product which the mayor recently endorsed in a TV commercial. Goodman's wearing a near matching French-blue shirt and a contrasting red silk tie. As I was told would be the case in advance, a mayoral aide sits in and dutifully tracks and notes our conversation.

Author Jim McManus, in his recently published Vegas-based *Positively Fifth Street,* suggested that at one point in his life, the mayor might have sat in on conspiracy to kill a federal judge. Goodman, roundly denying the charge, publicly fulminated that McManus was "some jerk" who never so much as interviewed him or asked him about the alleged incident. Totally in character, in the performance sense, Goodman had told the local media that if McManus, didn't apologize (as he eventually did) then he, the mayor, might have to "revert to my old baseball bat days."

So while historian, and Goodman admirer, Michael Green jokes that the "most dangerous place to stand in Vegas is between Oscar and a TV camera," the publicity-friendly mayor is taking a few more precautions nowadays with reporters and authors. Not to say that Goodman isn't his usual avuncular and straightforward self. Indeed, when on a couple of occasions his assistant wants to start winding down our chat, the mayor keeps it cranking. When we get around to the ongoing Galardi dance-club scandal Goodman says that "while just about every city is undergoing some sort of investigation" the possibility that Vegas city councilmen and county officials might be taking bribes "should not be considered business as usual."

"I believe that ethics has to come from within," he says, as a good former criminal lawyer. "Ethics are a personal and subjective matter. And if you do something that looks to someone else as unseemly, you know, that's not a crime. But if you cross the legal line, well, then you are a crook. If those activities are criminal those people should not be politicians. If, on the other hand, they are just exercising poor judgment, then they should not be voted back into office again."

If Goodman didn't exist as Mayor of Las Vegas, he would have had to be invented and installed somewhere on the Strip between the Mirage volcano and the Mandalay Bay shark tank as one more must-see attraction. "I think Oscar is the best mayor it's possible for Vegas to have," says historian Green, a critical but self-professed admirer of the mayor. "This town has been called the Second Chance capital of the world and Oscar embodies that. Las Vegas takes itself and Oscar Goodman at face value. And that's why he's so well-liked."

Born in 1939 to a middle-class Jewish family in West Philadelphia, Goodman's high grades got him into Haverford College and later through the law school of the University of Pennsylvania. After graduating he went to work for the appeals department of his hometown prosecutor's office—an agency where his father had worked. But after hearing tales about wild and woolly Las Vegas, Goodman came out here in 1964, with his wife Carolyn in tow and—he says—87 dollars in his pockets, and wound up working at different times for both the local prosecutors and the public defenders.

Goodman's career breakthrough, however, came in 1970 when he was hired to defend bookmakers in nineteen of twenty-six cities swept up in a federal phone-tap operation. Directly confronting the office of Richard Nixon's infamous attorney general, John Mitchell, and successfully arguing that the federal wiretaps were illegally authorized (in a weird omen of Mitchell's soon-to-come Watergate debacle,) Goodman won a stunning acquittal for all of his clients.

The young lawyer instantly became a favorite for "made" guys the government was trying to undo and found himself enlisted to represent a rogue's gallery of underworld superstars from Meyer Lansky, whom he helped free from a jam over casino cash-skimming, to Frank "Lefty" Rosenthal, to one-time feared Strip enforcer Tony "The Ant" Spilotro. Though Spilotro had been linked to twenty-two murders, Goodman kept his client out of jail and free—that is until 1986 when The Ant was crushed and beaten by rivals and unceremoniously buried in a Midwestern corn field. "Oscar is quick, he's bright, he's got a good feel for which way the wind is blowing," his former client Lefty Rosenthal, who now lives in Florida, told the local press a few years ago. "And he knows how to establish good powerful friends, which in the state you're living in is vital."

Yet, Goodman rankles with the oft-applied label of mob lawyer, insisting that only "5 percent" of his cases were gangster-related. "I'm proud of what I've done," he told the *Las Vegas Review-Journal* when he first ran for mayor in 1999. "If you can assure an unpopular person's rights are protected, the average person gets the spillover effect."

Goodman, a synagogue president, has never been charged with a crime, and his supporters point to the ample pro-bono work he's done on behalf of the poor. The National Association of Criminal Justice lawyers once hailed Goodman as "Liberty's last champion." His wife founded Las Vegas's leading private prep school and she and her husband are regulars at just about every local charity event.

But the mayor's popular support floats on the voters' conviction that as a straight talking multimillionaire he's too rich to be bought, his background too openly cheesy to allow him to be politically blackmailed or cowed, and that his sheer moxie, gumption, and motor-mouth provide the necessary push to keep downtown Las Vegas competitive, to earn the old city the respect it deserves, and to defend its interests as well as he did those of some of his earlier clients.

Goodman is an unlikely populist, tall and klutzy in his dark blue banker's suits, gray thinning hair and wire-rim glasses, but certainly a Peronista-like hero to the Vegas masses—thousands of whom I saw line up for a lavish free public buffet he threw under the lights of the Fremont Street canopy on the night of his landslide reelection this past spring. His admirers rushed up and crowded around him, not to shake his hand, but to hug and kiss him.

That Goodman has also brashly and shamelessly puffed himself into one more Vegas spectacle makes him even more popular and endearing. His supporters love the idea that one of the prized trophies in the mayor's old law office was a framed pair of steel balls given him by alleged mobster Charlie "The Moose" Panarella after Goodman risked jail by refusing to hand over client billing records to the cops. And they think it fabulous that their mayor can brazenly accept a starring role in a TV commercial for alcohol and then donate back the one-hundred-thousand-dollar fee to causes serving students and the homeless.

His refusal to apologize for Vegas or to pretend it's anything else but what it seems to be, at least in the consciousness of its millions of enthusiastic visitors, perhaps, wins him the most favor. And it also makes him talk like no other mayor in America would dare, even to his or her own priest.

Looking out his City Hall window at the sprawl below, he takes credit for being a vigorous "spokesman," if not precisely the author of the Las Vegas Convention Authority's highly successful and deliberately naughty "What Happens Here, Stays Here" national television ad campaign. "Las Vegas represents freedom, personal freedom," he says to me.

"People, particularly after 9/11, people who were rightfully down in the dumps know you can come here and do just about anything there is to be done as long as it is on the right side of the law. But you can go right to the cusp, OK?" he says with a slight smile. "And nobody bothers you, nobody tells on you. And then you can go home later to your mundane life and tell everyone you had a great experience out here, a lot of fun without worrying about being exposed. As far as I'm concerned, its like the old-time *omerta*."

His use of the mob term for the code of silence is hardly casual. It's part of Goodman's shtick and I'm one more journalist who, he guesses, will eagerly scribble that line into his notebook. And he's of course right—as well as overt about his own personal and civic marketing strategy. "You don't deny where we came from," he continues. "You build it up, you play with it, and you make fun of yourself—laugh with the mob, you know." When first running for office four years ago Goodman said: "People don't come here expecting to see Mickey Mouse behind a rock, but Bugsy Siegel." Vegas's mob connection, he said, should be fully capitalized on as a draw for tourists. "They like the excitement; if you try to detract from the past you're doing people a disservice." Now, Goodman wants to have a historic and unused downtown post office turned into a mob museum.

More serious campaign promises underpinned his initial 1999 election run, a candidacy that led the *Review-Journal* to editorialize "Anybody But Oscar." Goodman became the first candidate and eventually first mayor in a long time who openly talked about rectifying the city of Las Vegas's monumental mistake of never absorbing the lucrative Strip. He tells me he still wants to unify the two. "People don't really differentiate between the Strip and the city, it's all Las Vegas. And I'm the mayor of the *whole* valley as far as the world is concerned. And I do nothing to dissuade them of that idea."

That union seems unlikely. But what has surprised even many of his original critics has been the mayor's tenacious, dogged, and rather heroic fight to save and rejuvenate downtown Las Vegas. The entirety of his second term and what some say might or should be a possible run for the governor's post is staked on a precarious but ambitious downtown redevelopment plan.

Get him talking on this subject, and he soon sounds like a dreamy Jerry Brown who was elected mayor of Oakland on the same sort of urban vision. "I want an urban sophisticated district, an urban village," Goodman says of his downtown plans. Where ratty, weekly motels now abound, Goodman sees "a high-density residential zone, brownstones, lofts, for people coming here looking for community, where young professionals would live, doctors, lawyers, nurses, newspaper people, alternative newspaper people."

To jump-start this plan, Goodman had the city purchase a sixty-one-acre parcel on the edge of downtown, a plot which he calls the future "jewel of the desert." There he wants to anchor a diversified commercial center with a world-class academic medical center and a municipal performing arts center. For the future of the city, the mayor says, the project is do or die. And with Indian tribal casinos metastasizing along the highways that connect California to Nevada, downtown Vegas could be doomed. About half of the tourists who come to Vegas also come downtown and keep it viable. But the future remains cloudy.

"We can't have any near-death experiences," Goodman says.

"I'm extra worried about downtown, because I believe unless it becomes the gleaming, glistening place it was when I got here in 1964, with all the neon, glitz, and glamour we're gonna be sorely challenged by the Indian reservations."

Some critics think Goodman's plans have already failed and that the mayor is little but a self-promoting huckster. Other watchers take him much more seriously and point to some tentative patches of promising economic revival already taking root in the downtown checkerboard. The medical center idea is in negotiation with the Cleveland Clinic but not finalized. And the performance center is still on the drawing boards. The mayor can take credit for a new complex of 125 factory outlet stores just opening downtown, which are expected to draw 8 million visitors per year, and for a large furniture outlet scheduled to open in early 2005.

"I'm a fan of the mayor, I haven't written him off yet," says Geoff Schumacher, respected journalist and editor of Vegas's widest-circulation alternative weekly, *The Mercury*. "I think he's going to be successful downtown. He's the *only guy* who can do it, through pure stamina and arm-twisting. The city's never had a better mayor as its advocate."

Schumacher also argues that Goodman's quest to give Las Vegas a cultural heart downtown is desperately needed. "Vegas is not yet taken seriously as a major metropolitan area" he says. "For most people who come through it's still only the Bellagio or the New York New York and it's not the place where they want to set down roots. They think we all live in hotels, they have no idea what exists beyond the Strip and they don't care. Our cultural institutions are way behind our growth."

For all his zeal, Goodman commands a weak post. The Mayor of Las Vegas wields no more power than one of the other city councilman, and as he is constantly reminded, absolutely none over the almighty county-based Strip casinos and hotels to the immediate south. Mayor Goodman has more than once bitterly tasted their clout and jealous self-interest.

After his usual finagling, the mayor had finally enrolled officials of the NBA in the cause of bringing a professional sports team to Las Vegas, namely the Vancouver Grizzlies. Visions of a one-hundred-thousand-seat downtown stadium already danced in the mayor's head when he got blindsided by the Strip casinos. They had absolutely no intention, they said, of taking pro-basketball betting off the menu of their sports books, as the NBA would have required. Though some more cynical Las Vegans think that was just a flimsy excuse; maybe the casinos didn't want one more venue in town that could divert tourists from the slots and tables.

When the NBA plan got kiboshed, Goodman did something else few in Vegas dare: he publicly chided the casinos. Invited to speak to a banquet full of gaming executives, his opening line was that he was asked to speak about the contributions that casinos make to the greater community, but that he really didn't want to give only a ten-second speech.

As we are concluding our talk, Goodman says he has, since then, ironed out a better relationship with the Strip interests. Mostly because he has little choice. "They taught me a lesson and I learned it," he says with uncharacteristic humility. "The Strip casinos are the economic engine that drive this community . . . So I raised the white flag and not only do I have a speaking relationship with them, but the NBA idea is absolutely not dead."

Then Goodman pulls out one of his most-quoted standard lines. "I'm the happiest mayor in the country and I'll tell you why. It's so easy compared to being a criminal defense lawyer. If I made a mistake as a lawyer, there's no way to rectify it. But if I make a mistake as mayor I can put it back up on the agenda again."

I believe that Goodman is serious about downtown—just as I am convinced that he's telling the truth about being the happiest mayor. But the reasons he cites are obvious bullshit. Gamble, drink, get paid for booze commercials, pinch showgirl tushies, hang out with wise guys, say whatever the fuck you want, publicize all this and still and get nine out of every ten votes? Isn't that what every mayor only secretly dreams of doing?

Some bad news this very same night for Oscar and his plans. The MGM Mirage corporation says it's selling its famed downtown Golden Nugget and another Nevada property to a pair of former Internet businessmen for $215 million. When the deal is finalized later this year, there will be no major gambling corporation any longer operating in downtown Las Vegas.

The spic-and-span two-thousand-room Nugget, used two decades ago by Steve Wynn as the platform from which he launched his gambling empire, maintained Strip levels of luxury and continued to produce profits for it next owner, MGM Mirage, somewhere around twenty million dollars a year. But that apparently is not enough of a margin for the parent company that posts about an annual three hundred million dollars in earnings.

The mayor puts the best face on it, saying he's certain that the two thirty-four-year-old Web wizards, the former founders of *Travelscape.com,* who are taking over the property will give it the kind of care and commitment that will improve downtown. Perhaps. But, the transfer also undeniably means that the most powerful casino and hotel interests are simply giving up the downtown revival project.

For MGM Mirage, the Nugget sale is "a strategic move" which allows the corporation to bolster its balance sheet and to focus new investment in emerging gaming markets, says Chief Executive Terry Lanni in a corporate press statement. In other words, downtown is now experiencing the sort of pain and humiliation of globalization that pushed so many tens of thousands of economic refugees toward Las Vegas in the first place. Rather than continuing to invest, even profitably, in downtown Vegas, the corporate gambling giant is turning its back on its hometown in favor of a series of projects it hopes will produce even bigger gains: buying into Atlantic City's newest casino resort, negotiating to operate slot machine operations at New York's Aqueduct Race Track, and moving some operations offshore by purchasing a 25 percent share of Metro Casinos, a British corporation. Says a gaming industry analyst: "MGM Mirage is off to better and bigger things."

"Shame on the Homeless":
Private Prosperity—Public Poverty

N A CITY BRIMMING with professional lounge-show imperson-
ators of every stripe, where veritable legions of aging Ten-
nessee-toned Elvi trudge up and down the Strip futzing with
their hair, white leather suits and King-sized sunglasses, those
tourists who come upon forty-eight-year old David Buer probably don't give him a second look—no matter how incongruous
he looms against the background glitter.

When they spy him jumping into his dust-covered, small
Japanese car dressed in his soup-stained and torn brown
friar's hassock, the frayed rope belt around his waist, his
stretched leather sandals, his dirty blond pony-tail held in
place with a rubber band, and the placid, unflappable focus
of his pale-blue eyes peering out from behind smudged
glasses, they have to think that Brother David, as he's called,
is one helluva of a dead ringer for Jesus. That he must be

starring somewhere in some low-rent casino knock-off staging of *Jesus Christ, Superstar.*

But much to the chagrin of local officials, Brother David is much closer to the real thing than any simulacra. One of two Franciscan missionaries working in this city, David Buer is the undisputed *Generalissimo,* Strategist, Advocate, and Public Defender of Las Vegas's standing army of six or eight or ten thousand homeless. And in a city of supposed winners, of instant fortune and round-the-clock hedonistic abandon, he couldn't be more unpopular.

When I catch up with him, he's leading a monthly meeting of community activists and he's really pissed. In a quietly outraged tone, he reads out-loud from an article buried in that morning's page 11B of the *Review-Journal* about a just-released report from the National Coalition for the Homeless. Citing thirteen incidents of violence against the local homeless, including four deaths over the last four years, the report declares Vegas to be the second most dangerous city in America for street-dwellers, right after Denver.

Then, switching to a tone of mocking contemptuousness, Brother David reads Mayor Goodman's published reaction to the report. "They're full of hooey," the mayor says. "They say I'm harsh in my rhetoric. I tell the truth. You want to know how these people get hurt? They hurt each other. If you saw some of things they do to each other, you'd say, 'Shame on the homeless.' "

To a roomful of guffaws, Brother David slaps the newspaper down on the table in front of him. "Imagine that," he says. "Shame on the homeless? Better, shame on the mayor."

Brother David and the other activists aren't really that surprised. The mayor has already racked up quite a public record in his fulminations against the homeless. He once referred to them as "cockroaches." Another time he suggested they be rounded up and warehoused at an abandoned state prison a half hour out of town. Brother David tried to stand down city bulldozers in the summer of 2001, when scores of the homeless saw their makeshift tent city along the railroad tracks on the edge of downtown razed by the Vegas police. Ten months later, on Palm Sunday of 2002, Brother David was again in the front lines as the cops tore down their new encampment across the street and rousted the homeless a second time that same morning when they drifted toward a neighboring lot.

On just about any other day or night, some unit or another of the Metro police—a tough-knuckled, steely-eyed force reminiscent of Daryl Gates's LAPD—can be found hassling or arresting some unfortunate street people. When one local indigent stood on a corner and did nothing except hold up a makeshift sign reading "The Lord is My Shepherd" he found himself locked up and charged with panhandling. When Brother David led a protest march of the homeless under the Fremont Street Experience canopy, police threatened them again with possible charges of soliciting on private property—even though the canopy arches over a public thoroughfare. (In July 2003, a federal appeals court finally ruled that that the Fremont canopy is a public forum where all First Amendment–protected activities must be allowed. The city is appealing the decision).

Currently, the City of Las Vegas spends about two one-hundredths of a percent of its budget on the homeless. Brother David and his fellow activists have come up with a comprehensive plan that would increase that figure by ten-fold, to one-tenth of a percent. They'd also like to see the casinos and hotels take on the problem with some serious contributions of employment or funding. So far, they haven't gotten their calls returned from

America's chief gambling industry lobbyist, former Republican National Committee chair, Frank Fahrenkopf.

"The streets of Las Vegas are harsher than other places. We have a harsher mayor. And from the perspective of the homeless, things are getting worse—not better," Brother David says as we take a drive through the seemingly bombed-out patch of the city that everyone calls the Homeless Corridor. Near the old Fort Mormon, the Corridor stretches for four blocks, bridging the edge of downtown with North Las Vegas. Hundreds of homeless mill under the desert sun, drifting among the Corridor's few shelters and a gigantic Super Pawn store. "It's a major struggle just to meet the most basic needs here," Brother David continues. "Other places are more tolerant. Less so here because of its dependence on tourism." And the sources of homelessness here are more problematic. "You can be slaves to many things," he says. "Drugs, alcohol, or gambling. But they say you go through your money much faster with gambling than drinking."

The Crisis Intervention Center, a one-stop umbrella service center for the homeless, managed by Catholic Charities and sitting on land owned by the city, anchors the Corridor. "We want to change the name of this place to the Corridor of Hope," Brother David says as we pull up in front of the Center. But hope seems in short supply. Catholic Charities has announced it will soon discontinue providing free beds for the homeless. Because of the conditions attached to its grant funding, it will serve only homeless military veterans in the future. And even in the present, Catholic Charities displays what one counselor inside the center terms a "Gestapo attitude" toward the homeless.

Though no Las Vegan has fought harder for the homeless than Brother David, he—and I—are severely scrutinized, hassled, and pushed around in hostile, even threatening tones by the

Center's uniformed and armed guards—a force run by the former head of security of the Nevada Test Site. When we recount this to the counselor inside, he says: "This *is* Las Vegas, you know—a place without much compassion and humanity. What Brother David does around here is not a high priority. Even for Catholic Charities." When I ask Brother David how he accounts for such intemperance by his fellow Catholics, he smiles and says, "We pray for them." Pointing to the shelter facility itself, he adds, "Look at that. A beautiful, modern complex. One heavily patrolled all day just to keep people out."

At least on the southern limit of the Corridor, a more accommodating atmosphere is found at the 155 bed Las Vegas Rescue Mission, a fabulously clean and orderly shelter, struggling mightily to expand. With a new residential building, a clinic, a women's and family section, and serving the Corridor's main nightly meal to 350 or more, the Mission could use a budget of $1.5 million. But in this city swamped in billions of coins and chips tossed into machine and onto tables, the shelter can only raise half of its optimum budget.

"The casinos are very good to us," resident pastor Vince Motola says to me. He's such a sweet-tempered man, I frankly can't tell whether or not he's being sarcastic. "They give us food, the leftovers from the buffets. And sometimes they give us their unclaimed items from Lost and Found. They're not very good for giving money," he says with no emotion. "Never seen any money from the casinos."

Six years ago, out of desperation, Brother David founded Poverello House for the homeless, a "daytime hospitality center" in gritty West Las Vegas. Brother David and another Franciscan live directly across the street in a ramshackle courtyard apartment that the order has maintained in Las Vegas for the last thirty years. As Franciscans take a vow of poverty, their quarters have wooden floors, a wood-burning stove, and a fading portrait of Martin Luther King over the hearth.

A tiny, two-room converted wood-frame residence, equipped with a kitchen, a few bunks, a shower stall, a dining room table, a washing machine, and a sunburnt back patio with one tree and a plastic tarp for shade, Poverello House is about the only safe place in all of the city for the homeless. Only here can they spend the day free from threat of rousting. The demand is so great for the respite that the house offers that each guest at Poverello—which means "little poor man" in Italian—is allowed one day-time stay of eight hours once a week.

On the nearby skyline horizon, the glinting white and rouge downtown Lady Luck casino tower sneeringly reminds Poverello's clients just how fickle and heartless she can be. "Come here. Spend your money. Go home. Don't even look at the homeless," says one thirty-two-year old man lazing under the branches of Poverello's backyard tree.

The predicament of Vegas's homeless is only, perhaps, the most dramatic aspect of what historian Eugene Moehring calls Las Vegas's "private prosperity and public poverty." Vegas homeless services currently get more money from Washington than from local and state administrations. Consistently performing as America's most economically successful state, Nevada falls way behind in social and government services. By most economic analysts' reckoning, the Silver State has the second highest tax revenue potential in the union, yet the taxes it actually imposes are the third lowest in the country—making Nevada a great place to live, if you are very wealthy.

Nevada seems stuck in its past, not wanting to grow up,

avoiding the responsibilities of a state that grows faster than any other, driven, in turn, by America's fastest-growing metropolis. A deadly combination of the transient nature of much of its population (which feels little stake in the system), anti-tax and anti-government rural cow-town conservatives, and a state government in the thrall of the gambling industries pretty much guarantees that Nevada's services will continue to dangerously lag. What local columnist John Ralston calls "pathetically funded education" and "Third World assistance to the poor and mentally ill" has generated an infrastructure so rickety and so unappealing to outside investors that the state is failing in its long sought-after goal to diversify its economy away from gambling.

"Our already inadequate services are, to make things worse, also now under-funded," says Paul Brown, Las Vegas's chief liberal activist, referring to the budget shortfall Nevada, like forty-two other states in the union, is confronting this year. "In public education, we spend $1,100 a year less per student than Mississippi. We're thirty-eighth in the nation in health services. We have some of the highest rates of unimmunized children. We're fifty-first in Medicaid spending, behind Washington D.C. We have twice the national rate of suicide, and when you call the Las Vegas hotline it sometimes rolls over to phone answerers in Reno, hundreds miles north of here. And we are fifty-first in tax progressivity; we have the most regressive taxation in the nation."

Nevada is only one of five states without a general business tax, and while there is no state income tax, average residents get soaked by heavy sales and consumer taxes.

The cash- and profit-laden gambling industry contributes a huge share of Nevada's revenues by paying a 6.25 percent tax on its billions of dollars of take, and claims to be paying more than its way. So when it was obvious that Nevada was going to fall nearly a billion dollars in the red in 2003, the casino industry deftly, and a year ahead of the curve, put together a broad political coalition—including liberals, labor, and moderate Republican Governor Guinn—that proposed to finally impose taxes on other industries and businesses that have so far gotten a free ride.

But that was a disingenuous and deceptive strategy. Certainly Nevada's tax base needs broadening and other wealthy businesses should, indeed, start anteing up. The casinos, however, should also be paying much, much more. Yet, the very notion seems taboo. "The casinos are the nine-hundred-pound gorillas that everyone is politely ignoring," says an activist in the Culinary Workers Union who disagrees with labor's alliance with the gaming corporations on the tax issue. "If we taxed them the way we should, we'd have no deficits in Nevada. And what are the casinos going to do if we did that? Pack up and leave town? How do you pack up Caesar's Palace? The problem is a total lack of political will to soak the casinos by all those politicians they've bought up."

Contributing nearly a million dollars per election cycle, and spawning an incestuous revolving door between the industry and public service, the gambling interests exercise enormous influence over both major political parties in Nevada and hold virtual veto power over public policy decisions.

That clout has kept Nevada's politicians supine and the gaming tax frozen since 1987 at the lowest in the nation—except for California whose politically craven Governor Gray Davis signed agreements with Indian tribes that allows them to pay *no* state taxes. But compare Nevada's gaming tax of just over 6 percent with Mississippi which extracts 8 percent and as much as 11 percent in some jurisdictions from its infinitely less successful casinos. Atlantic City casinos pay more than a 10 percent levy to New Jersey. Other Eastern Seaboard states tax booming Indian casinos at up to 25 percent. And Illinois' new governor Rod Blagojevich wants to raise casino taxes from the national high of 50 percent to 70 percent. Some of the Vegas-based gambling corporations already pay some of these high tax rates on out-of-state casinos they operate.

Some polls show that two-thirds or more of Nevadans support a higher gambling tax. Yet the brutal state budget battle that divided the state and dominated all political discourse throughout 2003 broke along fault lines that spared the casinos. And that was hardly serendipitous.

Instead of debating the obvious, i.e., how much to raise gambling taxes along with imposing new levies on other industry, Nevadans found themselves lining up on opposing sides of a sterile, politically manipulated choice. The Republican governor, most of his party, the Democrats, and the casino industry were willing to hike taxes seven- to eight-hundred-million dollars and disagreed among themselves only on whether to impose a gross receipts tax or a payroll tax on business. On the other side, a small faction of rural Right-wing Republican legislators opposed the new business tax, instead wanting deeper cuts in social services, and held up any budget agreement for months. On July 1, 2003 the constitutional time limit for agreeing on a budget breached, the governor asked the state supreme court to intervene.

The governor's tax plan would have raised the gambling levy by a mere half-percent, a negligible increase that would only cover 5 percent of the shortfall and that was eagerly supported by the casino corporations.

One courageous and quirky politician given to cruising his

district in a big sedan with a ten gallon hat on his head, state senator and three-time Democratic gubernatorial candidate Joe Neal has been leading a lonely and quixotic fight to raise the gambling tax as much as four percent—an increase that in one simple blow would cover more than half the state deficit. An aging black man, a former casino porter and janitor who has represented impoverished West Las Vegas in the legislature for more than three decades, Neal has made the casino tax increase his obsessive cause. But his fellow Democrats are just as smitten, if not more, than the Republicans with their corporate gambling contributors, guaranteeing that Neal's measure dies in committee every time he raises it—though in the current budget jam, he got at least a smattering of support from some of the more gutsy among his colleagues.

No surprise that in his latest reelection bid Neal escaped political death by less than two hundred votes when the casinos lavishly bankrolled a younger rival, self-professed "business Democrat" Uri Clinton. Clinton, a lawyer who worked with the casinos, claims he won't run again in 2004. But a broad consensus of local pundits agree that the venerable Senator Joe Neal, the only elected official to make the Local Heroes list of Las Vegas *CityLife* magazine, remains in the sights of the casino and must be considered politically doomed. One can only assume that the gaming interests will now only redouble their efforts to bag the senator, after the sharp-tongued comments he made as his casino tax increase bill was most recently killed off.

Telling the press he was sure that the old Vegas gangsters would never have fought his bill as hard as the corporate gaming lobbyists did, he said Nevada could solve its record budget deficit more easily if the mob still controlled the casinos. "We don't want them back," Senator Neal said. "We just want the taxes. If the mob was in control, they'd say, 'Go ahead and tax me. I'll make it up somewhere else.' . . . When people from the church went down to talk with certain people," Neal continued, "they wrote you a check. If you had a charity function, they wrote you a check. They had money for that. But these corporations, they squeeze tight when it comes to money."

Senator Neal's acerbic and absolutely truthful remarks brought forth a laughable cascade of pious public disavowals and denunciations from both Republican and Democratic legislators, fumbling over each other to stress how far Nevada has come, how fortunate that state is now that the gaming industry is clean and regulated, and how nobody in their right minds would even think of a return of the mob.

Only the state senate's top Democrat, Dina Titus, spoke out in support of Joe Neal. She disagreed with him, she said, but she argued Neal was merely making the point that "corporations only care about the bottom line." No one should be shocked or surprised by Neal's comments, she said. "Are they surprised that we have a mayor in Las Vegas who was a mob lawyer and wants to set up a mob museum? Should they be?"

The Apostle:
Gambling Is Good

N O SOONER THAN HE was elected the new sheriff of Vegas in the fall of 2002, Bill Young started feeling about as spurned by the local powers-that-be as was fictional Police Chief Martin Brody in Steven Spielberg's classic, *Jaws*. Like his film world counterpart, Sheriff-elect Young had dared to touch the third rail of local politics and commerce. "If we have any terrorist attack in Las Vegas," Young told a conference of gaming executives, "we are done as the tourist Mecca of America. And being America's playground, we have to be a prime target for fundamentalists whose beliefs are radically different than ours."

Young wasn't giving away any secrets. Five of the nineteen highjackers who carried out the 9/11 attacks had been in Las Vegas shortly before the downing of the towers. Bunked into a sleazy motel, they also spent time checking out the wares at the

Olympic Gardens titty-club, perhaps previewing the seventy-two virgins that awaited them in the afterlife. Investigators have so far not determined if they were scoping out anything else while in town. Further, a federal court in Detroit is moving against four others charged with terrorism who allegedly had plotted violent attacks against the Vegas MGM Grand.

But the new sheriff was publicly pilloried, scolded, and lambasted for as much as mentioning the T-word. The casino corporations had already seen an avalanche of cancelled reservations when two recent terrorist alerts mentioned Vegas as a possible target. This commercial paranoia prevents the police from even boasting of their successes. "So if we actually prevent a [terrorist act], we won't be able to talk about it because reports in the news media will have an impact themselves," said Bill Conger, the Vegas Metro police commander for national security.

The September 11 World Trade Center attacks initially put an unprecedented crimp in Vegas's profits. People weren't so much afraid to come here as they were to board a plane. Weekday business plummeted in the wake of the attacks, and Vegas—traditionally immune to economic recession—was all of a sudden feeling a squeeze.

Taxi drivers and, yes, lap dancers, saw their incomes cut in half or smaller. In the city of eternal employment, as many as fifteen thousand casino and hotel workers, from maids to dealers, found themselves laid off. There were suspicions that some of the profit-hungry casinos were exaggerating the crisis, wringing as many concessions, doubling-up of shifts, speed-ups, and benefit cuts as they could from a defensive work force. "This is the new mindset," says Professor Bill Thompson of UNLV. "Terry Lanni, who runs MGM Mirage, actually lives in California. He thought nothing of laying off thousands after 9/11. That's the

New Vegas. The Old Vegas would have never done that. Sure, they would have put on the brakes, scaled things down, worked it out somehow with their people, but not laid them off."

Instead, for months after 9/11, a huge white tent stood in a parking lot near the Stratosphere Hotel—serving as a union-run emergency employment and food center for out-of-work families.

The Vegas economic crisis provoked by the 9/11 attacks was, by most other national measures, penny-ante. Business and profits dropped by a mere handful of points, at most. But to a city spoiled by four decades of nearly uninterrupted expansion and growth, it was an horrific experience. "We're in a new phase now in our history," says Thompson. "We're part of the United States of America after 9/11. We find we are actually dependent on Americans who are willing to fly here. We've lost our economic immunity."

The slow fading of the impact of 9/11 and the end to what the administration daintily calls the "major fighting" in Iraq, has greatly eased the Vegas crunch. There's no boom like the '90s. But the emergency tent is gone. Most if not all the furloughed workers are back on the job, although some with reduced hours. And most importantly to the corporate Mandarins, Vegas room rates are back on a continuous if slow rise—averaging more than one hundred dollars a night and peaking at three or four times that amount in the upper-scale hotels on premium weekends. In June 2003, The Mandalay Bay posted its highest quarter earnings—a gross of $615 million—since it opened four years previous. Mandalay Resort Group CEO Glenn Schaeffer buoyantly told his annual stockholders' meeting "The Strip is one of the few places where prices go up every year, absent a 9/11 or a war."

That sort of optimism in Sin City's future cautiously rippled through this year's American Gaming Summit held at Harrah's

Rio Hotel—the yearly confab of casino CEOs, consultants, industry bankers and anyone else willing to pay a registration fee of seventeen hundred dollars to hear two days of analyses and opinions from the top dogs.

As the bosses of MGM Mirage, Harrah's, Park Place and other casino conglomerates take the podium, sit on panel discussions, and press the flesh at the scheduled luncheons, they seem to be—and they are—the very epitome of American corporate culture. Here there's no playful genuflection to the dark past—I'm surprised they have even invited Mayor Goodman for a brief introductory speech.

What most comes out of these two days for me is the absolutely risk-averse nature of the pinched, little men who operate America's fattest gambling operations. Every possible variable is calculated meticulously. Only we customers take the risks. These casino executives are overwhelmingly conservative white men, most of them contributors to the 2000 campaign of George W. Bush—though Al Gore was considered to be more aggressively "pro-gaming."

Over the Gaming Summit's two days of proceedings, they fret over higher taxes, especially on them and their corporations; they ponder the expansion of Indian casinos, slot-machine "racinos," and Internet gambling. Torn over whether to oppose all the above or invest in them, they mostly lean to the latter. "We are in favor of only legal I-net gambling," says MGM Mirage CEO, Terry Lanni. "My view is simple: it's happening and therefore cannot be stopped. It should be regulated, licensed and taxed." But not too much, of course. In the meantime, MGM has already set up a Web casino from a site on the Isle of Man, ready to go full blast if legalized in the U.S.

The casino companies also know that cash-starved states

wallowing in red ink are increasingly looking toward expanding gambling venues—which is good. But the states also want to more heavily tax those revenues—and that's very, very bad. "We are concerned," says Lanni, "that state budget deficits will prompt higher licensing fees."

Center stage at the summit, however, is ceded to the man who might as well be called "The Apostle of Gambling." Dressed in a sharp pin-stripe suit, a yellow power tie, Italian loafers and a starched blue shirt with white collars and cuffs bolted with gold presidential links, and matched by a solid-gold Rolex, Frank J. Fahrenkopf cuts the figure of a stereotypical inside-the-beltway K Street lobbyist. Which, as President and CEO of the American Gaming Association, is exactly who and what he is. Fahrenkopf is American gambling's hired gun, the "national advocate for the commercial casino industry," as his official bio says.

Perhaps more noteworthy, Frank Fahrenkopf served as chairman of the Republican National Committee longer than any person in the twentieth century, until he retired in 1989. Back then he was a national advocate for the Reagan Revolution and for a GOP that was rapidly integrating and elevating its hard-right Christian conservative flank.

Making the transition from flack for the Moral Majority and the Christian Coalition to shill for three-card poker and Blazing-7s slot machines, though, has seemingly not been at all difficult for Fahrenkopf. Seeing him deliver the keynote speech to the gambling summit is to see the same old right-wing partisan operative, demonizing the same old list of punching-bag enemies. Just as he once argued that conservative Republicans and presumably their corporate backers were persecuted by an effete liberal establishment, the million-dollar-a-year lobbyist argues that the innocent, underdog gaming industry and its corporate backers are also persecuted by the same claque of radical tax-and-spend liberals. The *Washington Post* and the *New York Times* are still part of what Fahrenkopf says is the "socialistic media." Trial lawyers suing casinos on behalf of pathologically addicted gamblers are "the enemy."

Walking the banquet floor grasping a hand-held microphone, a sophisticated PowerPoint presentation flashes behind him and punctuates his canned speech. Lotteries are good, he says, "because they have funded schools and universities." Pari-mutuel betting is good, generating, he says, $3.76 billion in 2001. Racinos, those tracks with slot machines, they're good, too, Fahrenkopf says, providing 7,928 jobs in six states. "If you want to go into a state without a casino and put one in, you've got all sorts of problems," Fahrenkopf tells his rapt audience. "But when you say you just want to put some slots into the racetrack, you're talking about an already existing venue. You're just improving and helping out an aging industry."

I half-expect Fahrenkopf to utter out in Gekko-like fashion that "Gambling Is Good!"—with the same passion he brought preaching to trickle-down economics, he now spreads the gospel of gambling. "There's no connection between the gaming industry and bankruptcy" he proclaims. "Crime? It's not true that we contribute to crime . . . addiction, bankruptcy, and crime are just not created by gambling," he reveals to enthusiastic applause.

But as much as Fahrenkopf worries over what he calls "industry inhibitors," his biggest target remains—just as when he was RNC chair—taxes. "I'm a big Churchillian," he says with a chuckle. "I told a Churchill story six years ago and I think it is more apt today," he continues: "Churchill was defeated in 1945 by Labor leader Atlee. But at that time, the Labor Party was off the Left-edge of the world. Churchill was at one far end of a urinal and Atlee at another. 'My you're shy,' Atlee says. 'No,' says Churchill. 'It's just that when you see something big, you want to nationalize it.' Gaming was big six years ago. It's bigger now."

Fahrenkopf stretches out his talk, flailing some more at the *Post* and the *Times* and as his sermon subsides a thought occurs to me. Maybe I should have recorded it and, every time I feel tempted to gamble, play it back. The thought of any gambling profits filtering back to this right-wing poltical hack would be a much more effective deterrent—for me at least—then the earnest labors of Robert Hunter and Bo Bernhard at the Problem Gambling Center. I know I'm not really about to opt for abstinence. But I also know that for the rest of my life I will be haunted by Fahrenkopf, that any time I lose as much as a nickel at a Blackjack table, I will immensely regret supporting an industry that this tassel-loafered flim-flam man represents.

The one man who all agree will most influence the course of Vegas's future was conspicuously and ironically absent from the 2003 Gaming Summit. Steve Wynn sold off his sparkling Vegas casinos to MGM—now MGM Mirage—for $6.4 billion in 2000 and currently operates not a single casino resort.

But even as the first $650 million leg of a long-awaited monorail comes to fruition, as the upscale Bellagio, Venetian, and Mandalay Bay each scurry to add another one thousand rooms or more each, as the Planet Hollywood people try to transform the failed Aladdin Hotel and Casino on the Strip, all Vegas watchers have their attention focused on the corner of Las Vegas Boulevard and Desert Inn Road where Wynn is building the next, best thing.

Two years after he razed the tower of the D.I., and after a rocky but successful IPO, whose underwriters include the Bank of America, Deutsche Banc Securities, and Bear Sterns, which raised $790 million in one day, Wynn is putting $2.4 billion into building the only mega-resort that Vegas has dared to erect since the economic bump of 9/11. The new property, originally slated as "La Reve" is now to be called simply "Wynn Las Vegas," its principal owner announced in the summer of 2003 after his company conducted extensive market research and polling. "No one knows what La Reve means," Wynn says in a press statement. "No one knows how to pronounce it."

"Everyone knows what 'Wynn' stands for," he says. "It is a brand that already exists, but until now has remained behind the scenes. If ever there were a time to put a face on in the Wynn name it would be now." Or maybe, after the war in Iraq, Wynn got cold feet about using a French name.

Behind metal fences, with the help of a forest of cranes and whole armored divisions of earth-moving equipment, the new resort—to open in 2005—is finally, visibly emerging. Huge mounds of dirt are taking on defined forms. A concave orangish steel skeleton is rising floor by floor. On the 200-acre site of the former Desert Inn, an 8-story man-made "mountain" and 3-acre lake will sit in front of the new hotel's 2,700 rooms and 18 restaurants. A Ferrari and Maserati dealership will be among the high-end resort shops and the D.I.'s old championship golf course will be rejuvenated. And a joint being, in the end, always a joint, the Wynn Las Vegas will be no different, housing an ample casino with at least two thousand slot and video machines and a yet undisclosed number of card and craps tables.

With his resort-building legacy enshrined in the Mirage, Bellagio, and Treasure Island resorts, no one doubts that Wynn's latest venture will once again raise the bar of Strip luxury a notch higher. The only question is if Wynn Las Vegas will totally reset the market—the way his Mirage did in 1989.

The opening of the Mirage set off the New Vegas revolution that spread from the mid-Strip southward. But will his new resort, on the north end of the Strip, set off a second boom that will revolutionize the top half of Las Vegas Boulevard? The casinos neighboring or nearby Wynn's new venture include the faded and frayed Frontier, Sahara, and Riviera and the dramatic but ignored and low-end 1,100-foot Stratosphere—all of them ripe for billion-dollar makeovers.

But with the unemployment at record highs in the summer of 2003 and the economic recovery of a rather hollow sort, will people continue to come to Vegas as they had in the half century before 9/11?

Thanks in great measure to the success of Wynn's own strategies, only 43 percent of Strip revenues come from gambling, compared to 59 percent in the late '80s. Gamblers will always come to Vegas, but in economically uncertain times, what about the tourists?

As always, Las Vegas is taking few chances. Increased convention business is being aggressively sought and the Mandalay Bay just opened an entire new wing dedicated to conventions. Other resorts are now following suit. In another new trend Caesar's Palace spent $100 million to build a coliseum-like lavish showroom which Celine Dion is making her performance home for the next five years. Other top name entertainers are exploring similar deals with other hotels.

"Way back in 1955, *Life* magazine ran a big cover story asking if Las Vegas had been overbuilt," laughs UNLV's Bill Thompson. "But we have always found we can build more. Always have, always will. And the demographics support us. Every day in the U.S., ten thousand people turn age fifty."

That's an argument echoed by Philip Satre, the long-time chief of Harrah's, who told this year's gaming summit: "The demographics are in our favor. We depend on people with time and money more and more: baby boomers, with their kids out of the house and their mortgages paid down. And the boomer generation is very comfortable with us. It doesn't think going to a casino is a sin."

But it's not just the boomers, at least according to a summer 2003 poll commissioned by Frank Fahrenkopf's AGA. The survey, conducted by Democratic pollster Peter Hart and Republican Frank Luntz, says that 85 percent of Americans see casino gambling as an acceptable activity for themselves or for others, up from 79 percent in the previous year.

A towering 91 percent of those polled aged 21 to 39 agreed. The poll also found that 54 percent of Americans support the introduction of casinos into cities or states where they live. Almost two-thirds said they believe that casinos "bring widespread economic benefits" to other businesses in the region. But 33 percent disagreed with that idea, up 4 percent from the previous year. Some academic observers said the entire poll was suspect and slanted to appease the casino clients of the AGA.

Fahrenkopf, nevertheless, said the poll results show there's still work to be done by casinos to fully win over the hearts and minds of the American people. "We know we haven't done a very good job showing the benefits of casino gambling," he said, adding that industry chiefs are considering the launch of a massive national advertising campaign to further spread that message.

What Would Jesus Bet?

S O MANY PEOPLE HERE, especially those who care most about their city and community, make the same plea. Remember, they implore me, Las Vegas is much, much more than gambling, the Strip, the casinos. It's one-and-half-million people, they say, most of whom don't work in casinos, and many of whom have never even set foot on the Strip. I'm also reminded that there's a budding cultural movement, a new Vegas Valley Book Festival, even an admirable Writers in Asylum Program based at UNLV and underwritten by Mandalay Resort Group chief Glenn Schaeffer, himself a brainy product of the Iowa Writers Workshop.

These are truths often overlooked, certainly by most of the weekend tourists who never venture off the Strip, except maybe for a short casino run downtown. But however complex and varied are the greater and outer layers of the Vegas universe, its sun and moon, its heart and soul, its very reason for being always reduces down to gambling. Take away the casinos and the businesses that service them, and Vegas—if not Nevada itself—would become one more parched patch of the Sun Belt struggling for attention, investment, and jobs with little to offer except low wages and lax environmental laws.

"Of the 50 largest employers in Nevada, 34 are casinos, one is a manufacturer of gambling devices, 11 are governments or their subsidiaries (school districts, police departments, post office), three are hospitals and one is a bank," Chuck Gardner, a former state deputy attorney general, wrote in the *Las Vegas Mercury* a few years back. "Five casinos are larger than state government. Of the largest 18 private companies in the state, all 18 are casinos. Of the 50 largest employers in [Las Vegas'] Clark County, 34 are casinos. Of the remaining 16, 11 are governments or their subsidiaries. The other five are the telephone company, a hospital, a bank, a convention service and a linen supplier, the last two serving the casinos almost exclusively."

So while those all-dominant casinos may still offer job opportunities difficult to match anywhere else in America, at least for relatively unskilled workers, Las Vegas hardly looms as the New Detroit, as the model for a new phase of national development. "I don't think Las Vegas is leading urban America into the future," says historian Eugene Moehring. "Our economic base of development is very narrow, we've failed to broaden it as much as we should have. We've got the biggest dam in the world thirty miles from here, a great university, but industry went to Phoenix, Tucson, and New Mexico instead. UNLV didn't even have an engineering department until 1985 because our business people were Little Leaguers.

"In that sense, Las Vegas is not the future of America,"

Moehring continues. "It probably had its biggest national impact back in the '60s when it allowed Atlantic City to open up for gambling."

Maybe not a model for development. But in uncertain economic times, Vegas remains a formidable population magnet. Even without a broad economic base, even if it means working in a casino or indirectly servicing one, the domestic migration toward Las Vegas continues unabated, recently raising median house prices in the surrounding valley to over two hundred thousand dollars. In the summer of 2003, as national unemployment hit a nine-year high, the total inventory of new houses ready to be owner-occupied in Las Vegas was, nevertheless, no more than sixty-eight among the top ten home-building companies. Those wishing to buy in the more desirable areas had to sign on to long waiting lists for available homes.

And the most desirable, the most sought after addresses among all the Vegas neighborhoods lay twelve miles and often a grueling mind-numbing freeway crawl northwest from the Strip in a breathtakingly beautiful desert valley whose rich mineral content sparkles a fiery orange and red under the always present sun.

Built on an original 22,500 acres acquired by Howard Hughes in the 1950s and named for the billionaire's mother-in-law, Summerlin is today a thirty-six-square mile, master-planned community, wholly owned by the Howard Hughes Corporation, making it one of the largest pieces of developed land near a major metropolitan city under a single owner. When fully completed a decade from now, thirty perfectly charted-out and planned "distinct villages" will house 160,000 people. It's current population is about 50,000. Though it originally languished, a partnership with the Del Webb corporation, and hundreds of millions of dollars in private and public investment in infrastructure, have turned Summerlin into *the* place to live in Vegas.

Like a finely detailed movie set, or model train landscape, everything has been thought of, provided for and given a place in Summerlin. Nevada's first tri-level freeway exchange flows into miles more of roads, multiple golf courses, seventy acres set aside for schools, including a variety of private religious academies, a performing arts center, the home of the Nevada State Ballet, and a strictly politically correct offering of diverse houses of worship.

Summerlin is what's meant by the phrase "a picture perfect post-card community." Perhaps too perfect. Driving its sprawling, winding maze of streets—defiantly and lushly land-scaped against the desert elements—I weave through a collection of linked, mostly-gated communities that range from the $150,000 "starter" homes in "The Arbors" village to the million-dollar-plus mansions that line the $35,000-a-year tournament championship country club. Jogging trails, pristine parks, Little League diamonds, a gleaming library, church steeples, and syna-gogues sparkle along the roadside. Commerce is confined to strictly zoned self-contained shopping villages and the Starbucks overflows on Saturday mornings with the locals in shorts and sweat clothes lazing over the morning paper, their leashed collies taking refuge in the shade of the patio tables. Could the woman sitting next to me possibly hail from Stepford or Sim City 3000?

Summerlin reminds me of a story a British war correspon-dent, Henry Reuter, told me when we were both covering the 1973 Yom Kippur War from the bar at the Cairo Hilton. One of the few Brits based more or less permanently in Nairobi, Reuter was asked by the American manager of a local luxury hotel to give his opinion on the property's new English-style pub and restaurant, aptly named Victoria Station.

After being served a plate of British bangers and a couple of pints of Guinness, the manager asked Reuter if, indeed, this wasn't a perfect reproduction of a London pub.

Looking at the elite dining crowd of fellow journalists, diplomats, and foreign businessmen, Reuter tartly replied: "To be honest, it's *almost* perfect. The one difference is that in a real pub in London, you'd probably find many more black people than I see here."

So it is with Summerlin, a *Poltergeist* in Paradise. So painstakingly pieced together to evoke a metropolis of conglomerated villages that it winds up negating the sense of any city at all. The entire development is constructed to deny not only that all this precious suburban splendor is a direct product of the dyspeptic, clanging, garish, smoky and ultimately sleazy Sin City just down the Parkway, but that Las Vegas, as such, even exists. Not to speak of the corporation that owns the development—a company that at one time tried to buy up and operate most of the casinos in town and had no problem deploying a battalion of mid-level hoodlums to run the joints it already owned.

Summerlin's master-planned zoning has barred strip-malls, billboards, and even most commercial advertising from this private oasis. Gambling is confined to one middle-sized casino on the edge of the development and to the bowels of the gargantuan J. W. Marriott hotel nearby. It's possible to live an entire life in Summerlin and pretend that you're somehow disconnected from, untouched, and untainted by an economy that thrives on legal bordellos, millions of handbills advertising illegal call girls, and casinos that shake out a net win of ten billion dollars a year from house-biased games. If you're putting in a backyard pool, just make sure you don't dig too deep.

All of which makes Summerlin the most American of all our

neighborhoods. It most successfully and safely compartmental-izes the way we live, "our lifestyle," and distances it from the way we actually make our livelihoods. Shutter the Vegas casinos and dance clubs, shut down the escort services and the legal whorehouses, and somnolent Summerlin would go the way of other Nevada ghost towns like Rhyolite or Chloride and dis-solve into dust.

I'm certain that it's by no accident that the National Absti-nence Clearinghouse Conference—a fancy name for the ultra-conservative American virgins' movement—has chosen the brand-new, antiseptic Summerlin Marriott as its convention site this summer of 2003. Someone must have told the organizers that, in spite of the modest casino in its belly, the Marriott isn't really Las Vegas, or, at least, that Summerlin is as far away from the demonic Strip as you can comfortably get and still somehow be in Las Vegas.

From across America, 750 members of the Christian-domi-nated organization that promotes sexual abstinence outside the bounds of holy matrimony have converged here with the explicit mission of rescuing the heathen. "What better place to bring this than Sin City?" asks a young participant who's come all the way from the windy plains. For three days the participants will stage and attend seminars on the history of abstinence, the consequences of premarital sex, the "myth" of safe sex, the false security of con-doms, and in celebration of the convention's theme: "Beyond the Neon: Creating a Culture of Character."

The conference's media director, Kristin Scuderi, explains why Vegas has been targeted for salvation. "Las Vegas is home to many children and has the sixth largest school district in the nation," she says. "Our mission is to promote sexual purity until marriage." In town and at the convention today, ready to hammer home that message, is fervent right-wing and anti-abortion former Nebraska congressman Jon Christensen and his wife, Tara Dawn Christensen, the former Miss America 1997 who got a rush of publicity when she claimed she was a 26-year-old virgin on her wedding night. Also on hand is the virgin movement's favorite ideologue, Robert Rector, an obnoxious, dweebish wonk from the conservative Heritage Foundation. Back in 1995 Rector helped engineer "reform" of Title V welfare programs by forcing recipients to undergo pro-abstinence propaganda sessions. Rector, as usual, will be speaking on what he argues is the link between American poverty and rates of casual sex, based on the dubious assumption that the rich only screw their spouses.

Running this show is the Clearinghouse founder, the blonde, lethally perky Leslee Unruh, a mother of five from Sioux Falls, South Dakota who flits nervously around the proceedings and chortles out orders in an electric-blue running suit. "We're here to bring hope," she tells me, squeezing my wrist in a death grip. "Isn't Las Vegas the city of second chances? Well, we're all about second chances, you know. Just because you're having sex, doesn't mean you have to continue."

The climax, if you will, of this year's meeting, however, will come later tonight, when two busloads of virgins, "secondary virgins" (those recovering their lost virginity), and some of their proud mothers, fathers, and supporters will take a couple of buses over to the Strip. Once there, the virgins plan to compete with the usual blizzard of handbills that advertise topless clubs, dance clubs, escort services, and private adult entertainers by passing out so-called "Good Girl" cards. The portraits of a half-dozen of these still-pure girls along with a web site address are on one side of the card. On the back of the card is the blatantly false and dangerous message reading: "There is no scientific evidence that condoms prevent the transmission of most sexually transmitted diseases including chlamydia, syphilis, chancroid, trichominiasis, genital herpes and HIV."

In the meantime, a couple score of pro-abstinence exhibitors hawk their wares to the registered convention-goers, and the odd noncombatant or two who stumble, incredulously and by accident, into the Marriott banquet rooms. For sale among the booths are hardback copies of *Kinsey: Crimes and Consequences,* white unisex boxer shorts with a red "Stop!" sign over the crotch, and glittering, lavender plastic tiaras to be worn on the heads of Virgin Princesses.

Turns out that a lot of the adults present here also staff what are called Crisis Pregnancy Centers—conservative-run outfits that advertise as abortion counselors and then pressure their young clients into keeping their unwanted children. Handsome, middle-aged Paulette Tracy who works at one such place, the All Women's Health Center in Binghamton, New York, tells me she's never been in Las Vegas before, but has come "out of personal experience."

"I ended up getting pregnant out of high school and gave the baby away and have always regretted my decision," she says. And then adds: "And then there's the generational curse, my teenage daughter also got pregnant. But," she says smiling, "she has kept it and we're raising the child."

Paulette's planning to help pass out the Good Girl cards on the Strip later tonight and she's not quite sure what to expect, she tells me. "Before I go out tonight, I will pray," she says. "The Lord Jesus is going to prepare the hearts of the people who will receive our cards and that will work. They *will* receive what I give. They will receive it well."

When the kickoff "youth rally" starts that evening at the Marriott, aimed at revving up the Virgin Princesses and Princes before they go out to leaflet the Strip, I find surprisingly few of those young virgins in sight. At least half, maybe even two-thirds of the crowd of five hundred, gathered under a huge banner reading "President Bush, Thank You for Supporting Abstinence Until Marriage," are actually adults. Chatting with them, many of them appear to be angry adults, resentful of a popular culture that defiles their cherished family values. On this they agree with Frank Fahrenkopf, that the American media, and the American cinema, and the American recording industry and, yes, the American public educational establishment and probably half the U.S. Congress are Godless Socialists.

The rally inside a Marriott ballroom is a painful, noisome event. Regardless of its expensive staging and high-tech special video and sound effects, after five or ten minutes it becomes as burdensome as an amateurish high-school play. When an Elvis impersonator ambles onto stage and stiffly mouths a pro-abstinence homily, I pull the plug and walk out.

The least I can do to counter all this, I figure, is to kill time before tonight's leafleting on the Strip—which I don't want to miss—by making a contribution to the Marriott's casino. Pushing the horrible image of Frank Fahrenkopf out of my head, I march out of the convention center and settle in at a basic rip-off multi-deck Blackjack table and, once again proving that luck trumps all, unwittingly and with no special effort turn my one-hundred-dollar buy into nearly five hundred dollars within an hour. Now I really feel superior. Not only have I denied the American Gaming Association clients any further profit, but I've also taken four bills from the hotel that hosted the virgins convention. My recent doubts about gambling are starting to clear.

I've been looking at the Mirage's artificial volcano for a good ten minutes before the two busloads of primary and secondary virgins finally disembark into the Siegfried and Roy Plaza, as this mid-Strip spot is called. About seventy-five have arrived and they take up their positions along the sidewalk, ready to pass out thousands of their Good Girl cards. If it weren't for the lights of the TV cameras and the flashbulbs of still photographers (the local media having a predictable feast at the expense of the Vegas virgins except for one exceptionally bone-headed and fawning column by Susan Snyder in the *Las Vegas Sun*), I'm not sure how much of a notice the Good Girls might actually get. At 9 P.M. on this Friday night, it's still about ninety degrees and a fairly stiff breeze blows along the sidewalks, swirling and mixing the literal tens of thousands of other handbills that entice with promises of "full service . . . discreet . . . very petite . . . very private," and so on. The Good Girls have to compete with brigades of Mexicans, Salvadorans, and Guatemalans—most in yellow or red T-shirts and ball caps who, having braved the Rio Grande and eluded the Migra, now etch out new lives in the promised land by expertly and noisily slapping forests-full of salacious cards, brochures, and fliers into the hands of the thousands of foot-dragging, beer-and-margarita swilling, fanny-packer Strip walkers who swarm and stream like a strange race of overweight ants.

The Good Girls seem to be targeting mostly other girls with their handouts, especially those they clearly deem as more visibly slutty, those in the shortest skirts and barest midriffs. The reception given the virgins' cards is less than overwhelming. Certainly not the divinely inspired sort of acceptance predicted to me a few hours earlier by the prayerful Paulette Tracy. Most recipients take one quick glance at the cards and toss them to the ground alongside those for the hookers, dancers, and escorts. Others brush back the cards with a wave of their hands. For all the effect these Good Girls cards are not having, the assembled virgins might as well be pissing into the roar of the volcano's waterfall behind them. One young male passerby takes a card from a teenage virgin, stops dead in his tracks, reads the front of the card, and says to the leafletter: "Cool! Do good girls cost more?"

Vegas, tonight, is definitely Mudsville for the young soul rescuers from the National Abstinence Clearinghouse. Yes, some school districts in Texas have given them grants to teach the evils of sex in public tax-payer supported schools. And, yes, some of the member groups are lining up for a bite out of the fifteen-billion-dollar funding pie their friend, President Bush, has earmarked for what he calls global AIDS education. But in bringing their crusade to Vegas, the virgins have both grossly miscalculated and revealed their political naïveté.

Rail all they wish about elite, liberal, secular humanist degradation of culture, but identifying Las Vegas as its capital is a monumental misreading. In fact, the Vegas Strip, with its kaleidoscopic, pulsating, neon-lit, spinning carousel of earthly delights, offering a guilt-free at-hand menu of indulgences, from the nickel slots to the thousand-dollar-an-hour nudie club VIP rooms, constitutes modern America's highest expression of the same unfettered, profit-driven, free market that these pristine conservatives and their ideological generals from the Heritage Foundation worship and extol. Do they think it only serendipitous that Mr. Fahrenkopf once headed an international federation of social-conservative political parties and that he remains a close ally of the same George W. Bush whom they so profusely thank for his mumbled platitudes in favor of chastity? Or that their own blustering morality czar, William Bennett, has been revealed as one more zoned-out and hopelessly addicted video slot-machine junkie? Or that the casino bosses funnel millions in political contributions to the same claque of tax-cutting, right-to-life politicians these virgins and their families go out and knock on doors for at election time? Don't these cultural warriors comprehend that their prospects are doomed? That even their Lord Jesus would stand bedazzled, transfixed, and ultimately paralyzed if confronted by the awesome power of the mocking corporate golden calves that so voraciously and insatiably graze along this Boulevard?

No place more, and more effectively, than this Spielbergian Rouge City churns the panoply of immediate desires and promises to instantly gratify them, even concocting new ones as quickly as the numbers appear on the roulette wheel scoreboard, shamelessly pandering to the lowest common denominators of human experience, those which—precisely—Adam Smith identified as "envy, pride, and ambition," not to mention the true lubricant of the market, greed. Not godless socialists, but rather the pin-striped mandarins of the S & P 500 who now run this place, are those who have engineered staggering economic, commercial, and entertainment expansion while at the same time bulldozing history itself, blowing to the wind even any pretense of spiritual values—the scrubbed, air-conditioned, and master-planned churches of pious Summerlin notwithstanding. No force on Earth so mercilessly flattens traditional values, uproots community, and creates its own self-referential *Matrix*-like world of commercial exchanges than the unbridled sweep for profit. A hundred and fifty years ago, Marx and Engels described the omnipotent destructive force of unchained capitalism. And though they wrote long before the system was supercharged with multinational corporations, junk-bond financing, and leveraged buyouts, they seemed to have the image of a pagan Las Vegas in mind, replete with gigantic hotels tumbling down to make way for the new, when they depicted the earthshaking effects of surging, unstoppable, capitalist development as: "All fixed, fast-frozen relations, with their train of ancient and venerable prejudices and opinions, are swept away. . . . All that is solid melts into air. All that is holy is profaned." Americans herd, almost instinctively, to Vegas to enter into this devil's bargain, flocking together every weekend in a secular Hajj, walking circles around the massive electrified totems of materialism that line the Strip. If their lives are to be ever more dominated by distant corporate employers and indifferent HMOs, if the voice on the other end of the phone is more and more frequently a soulless digital reproduction, if the baselines of the weekday workaday game are constantly shifted or erased and the books are cooked to favor the faceless Members of the Board, then why not—as Mayor Goodman counsels—escape for a weekend into the anonymous, nonjudgmental pay-as-you-go hedonism of Las Vegas? Here, at least, the balm of simulated radical individualism—detached and suspended in time for a night or two or maybe three from the daily hypocrisies and strictures of family, community, workplace, and church, with the notion that the undulating girl on your lap might really desire you, or that the dealer really wants to be your friend, and the lure of Blackjack paying three-to-two or that a royal flush might dump four thousand silver dollars in your lap—can salve the ache of nine-to-five powerlessness and alienation. In the only American city where all the bare-knuckle rules are posted and agreed upon, where the house advantage is recognized and flaunted, a regular guy's got almost an even chance of winning something. Amidst the belching volcano, growling white tigers, the splashing dolphins, the boom of the pirate's cannons, the roar of the animated F-16s streaking along the Fremont Street canopy, the splash of the New York New York harbor fireboats, the screech of the roller coaster atop the Stratosphere, and the rising resonant human hum of the always-present fanny-packers, sharpies, and hustlers, the high-rolling whales, the winners, losers, the lost and the dazed, well, among them the Good Girl virgins couldn't possibly be anything more than just one more part of the show.

Epilogue:
July–October, 2003

MUCH MORE THAN THE 115-degree temperatures made Las Vegas sizzle this past summer.

A national advocacy group held a press conference under the downtown Fremont Street Experience to announce it was now ranking Las Vegas the "meanest" city in America when it comes to dealing with the homeless.

The Washington, D.C.-based National Coalition on Homelessness included its condemnation of Vegas in its new report "Illegal to be Homeless: The Criminalization of Homelessness in the United States."

As the coalition prepared to give its statement, Vegas activists led by Brother David Buer sang and held banners calling for more shelters.

The coalition cited remarks by Mayor Oscar Goodman, his endorsement of downtown "sweeps" and the net loss of shelter space for the homeless over the past couple of years as factors that put Las Vegas atop the list.

"We believe, just as the mayor, that there should not be homeless people in this community. But, if those dollars used to criminalize them through sweeps and putting them in jail were instead used for housing, we wouldn't see the numbers of homeless people out here," said Donald Whitehead, the coalition's executive director.

"The big picture, for anyone who has been paying any attention, is that there is a pattern and practice of abusing and harassing homeless people with the intention of making them invisible, because that's what's good for business," said Gary Peck, executive director of the American Civil Liberties Union of Nevada. "We should be ashamed Las Vegas was chosen as the site for this report because of its horrendous record," Peck said.

True to his well-established public style, Mayor Goodman offered up no apologies. Instead, he said Las Vegas has done more than any of the valley's other cities to tackle homelessness in Southern Nevada. "I am not the meanest mayor," Goodman said. "I am the kindest, most gentle soul who ever sat in this chair."

Yet, the mayor added, "We are intolerant of those who don't follow the basic rules to get help, like leaving behind booze and drugs. We will help those who are mentally ill, those who need and want our help."

Some important progress had been made, meanwhile, on the fate of personal freedom and civil liberties in Las Vegas. The homeless coalition was able to hold its denunciatory press conference under the privately-owned downtown Fremont Street canopy because just a few weeks before, the Ninth U.S. Circuit Court of Appeals in San Francisco ordered that all free-speech rights be restored in that part of the city. The Fremont Experience may indeed be privately operated, the court ruled, but it was nevertheless built on a public thoroughfare, a venue in which the First Amendment was still fully in effect. City officials—who had earlier banned political activity under the canopy—tried to spin the ruling in their favor. But the *Las Vegas Mercury* editorialized that City Hall ought to just concede that it was "being beaten like a red-headed step child" by the Federal courts.

ACLU chief Gary Peck was delirious over the ruling, only the latest in a cascade of court opinions opening up more public space in Vegas. "I think overall it is fair to say that it's a new era in Vegas," he said. "It's no longer the case that whatever the government and the hotel-casinos want, they get with respect to the First Amendement . . . It's pretty evident they can no longer thumb their nose at the Constitution and trample on people's free speech. That's not going to cut it anymore."

The courts also handed down a few more decisions that promised to rattle Las Vegas, if not the entire state of Nevada. The Nevada Supreme Court ended nearly six months of bitter and stalemated debate in the state legislature when it ruled that requiring a two-thirds majority to pass the annual budget was unconstitutional. Republican Governor Kenny Guinn's compromise tax-raise of $836 million, supported by most Democrats and all but the most recalcitrant conservative Republicans, finally became law. No sooner was the ink dry when right-wing fringe groups announced plans to recall the governor. With the casinos and much of the political establishment standing firmly with Guinn, no serious political observer expected the recall to prosper. "All of us in Nevada have better things to do with our time and resources," ruled MGM Mirage chief Terri Lanni.

The same supreme court also decided by split-decision in

mid-July to overturn the murder, robbery, and burglary convictions of Sandy Murphy and Rick Tabish, who were convicted in the 1998 death of Ted Binion. The court ordered a new trial for both defendants, assuring a full-employment act for TV tabloid reporters who will now have to choose between covering this retrial or the emerging Kobe Bryant spectacle.

The majority court opinion said that the original trial judge erred by allowing Tabish to be tried on extortion charges not directly linked to Binion's death, along with the other charges. Legal experts following the case said the two defendants, still being held behind bars, had little if any chance of winning acquittal in the new trial.

The Binion family's stake in downtown went dramatically dark on January 9, 2004 when law enforcement barged into the fifty-two-year-old Horseshoe casino and shut it down. As stunned gamblers looked on, marshals seized about a million dollars to satisfy debts owed to union trust funds. Thus ended Becky Binion Behnen's—old Benny's daughter—five-year ownership of the Horseshoe. Four days later she sold the Nevada rights to the Horseshoe brand to the Harrah's corporation, guaranteeing when it re-opens that it will be but a mock imitation of its old self.

The G-string political scandal snapped back into the news, and with a vengeance. In mid-August, news reports confirmed that former Clark County comissioner Erin Kenney was formally listed as a defendant in the sealed federal probe of the Galardi lap-dance empire. The same reports said she was actively cooperating with the criminal investigators and it was anybody's guess who might get ratted out. It seemed Democrat Kenney had little choice in the matter other than to become a snitch.

A *Las Vegas Review-Journal* investigation revealed that while sitting as a county commissioner in 2002, Kenney made at least eighty-nine phone calls to strip-club lobbyist Lance Malone during the eight month period in which the commissioners were fashioning new lap-dance rules. Other reports revealed that Kenney had been caught on other intercepted phone conversations making plans to bank two hundred thousand dollars in offshore accounts.

Kenney's turning state witness undoubtedly gave the criminal probe new vigor. Two weeks after her cooperation with authorities was reported, federal authorities indicted strip-club owner Mike Galardi and his bagman, and former county commissioner Lance Malone on bribery charges. The charges arose not from happenings in Las Vegas, but rather in San Diego, where Galardi also operates a high-profile dance club.

Malone pleaded innocent. But Galardi, like Kenney before him, also cut a deal with the Feds and pleaded guilty to charges that he bought the votes of three San Diego city councilmen in an effort to overturn a law passed in 2000 imposing "no touch" rules on in city lap-dance clubs. The ordinance was similar to the measure passed two years later in Las Vegas's Clark County. In pleading guilty, Galardi said he paid bribes to the three San Diego city council members as well as tens of thousands to a police officer who would tip off the club when undercover vice agents were due to conduct inspections.

Apparently much of the bribe money that Galardi funneled to the San Diego city council orginated in Las Vegas and was camouflaged as campaign contributions. The *Review-Journal* has a list of at least thirty Las Vegas-area residents who contributed to the San Diego camapigns. They are all likely suspects for further investigation. Vegas politicians should also be concerned what kind of deal Lance Malone might eventually cut to get off the hook. As the go-between for Galardi, he presumbably knows where all the bodies are buried. The convicted Galardi is also in the process of selling off two of his Vegas clubs, including the fifteen-million-dollar Jaguars.

Finally, on October 24, 2003 Mike Galardi pleaded guilty in Las Vegas to federal racketeering charges. Two weeks later, a federal grand jury formally convicted Clark County Commissioner May Kincaid-Chauncey and former Commissioner David Herrera and Lance Malone for allegedly accepting bribes from Mike Galardi in exchange for political favors.

Meanwhile, prosecutors revealed that the investigation of Galardi was the first use of the USA Patriot Act—legislation that the White House said was intended to fight terrorists, not crooked strip club operators.

The no-touch rule remains on the books in San Diego. Inviting the same sort of corruption that has swamped Vegas, the sex sheriffs on the Los Angeles City Council this past summer enacted its own clampdown on the burgeoning lap-dance industry. But after club owners gathered enough signatures to place a repeal of the law on the ballot, the L.A. City Council reversed itself.

Federal authorties have yet to levy any formal charges against the other Vegas lap-dance king, Rick Rizzolo, whose Crazy Horse Too was raided and searched in early 2002. The feds are probing charges that Rizzolo is a front man and money launderer for a Chicago mob outfit. But an important civil suit against his club has finally been scheduled for early 2004. The suit was filed two years ago by Kansas City resident Kirk Henry, alleging that a club employee attacked him in the parking lot and left him paralyzed. Henry alleges that his neck was broken by one of Rizzolo's bouncers after a dispute over a bar tab. Once on the ground, Henry says, another bouncer stole money from his wallet.

The unfolding G-string scandals have had no effect on the city's lifeblood: the gambling industry. Slot machine giant International Game Technology unveiled its newest electronic money vacuums at this summer's Global Gaming Expo in Las Vegas. The new devices included machines based on *The Dating Game* and *The Newlywed Game*. IGT's vice-president of game design, Joe Kaminow says his company picked the two Chuck Barris-created TV shows as themes because of the abundance of video and audio stock available, and because of the opportunities both games provide for player interaction.

Perhaps the most anticipated of the new IGT devices is the *Terminator* slot machine, featuring Arnold Schwarzenegger. The machine was made possible only after the April settlement of a lawsuit brought by the Austrian-born star against IGT in 2001 alleging improper use of his likeness, voice, and image. IGT has not yet announced when or where the new *Terminator* machines will be deployed. But they are likely to appear long before Schwarzenegger completes his new term as governor of California. The *Terminator* would be the first slot machine in history to be based on a sitting elected official, or any former elected official for that matter.

There were some other anecdotal indicators this summer as to where Vegas is now headed both economically and culturally, if any such distinction can be drawn. The defintive death of Vegas as a kid-friendly resort was marked by the late September auctioning-off of pirate-themed memorabilia from the former Treasure Island resort and casino, heretofore to be known as simply the T.I. Among the paraphernalia put up for bid by the

MGM Mirage holding company are two all-bone chandeliers originally valued at four hundred thousand dollars each.

That Vegas's marketeers had decided that its Nice Vice strategy was the most successful of its appeals and that the old twin standbys of sex and gambling would always be the city's strongest allures was confirmed when reports surfaced that attempts to showcase fine art on the Strip were seriously faltering. Steve Wynn had brought high art into the Vegas mix in 1998 when he spent three hundred million dollars to stock his new gallery in the just-built Bellagio. But attendance at the Bellagio gallery has reprotedly dropped from three thousand visitors a day when it first opened to as few nowadays as seven hundred fifty. The Guggenheim Las Vegas based at the Venetian Hotel recently closed due to a similar customer shortage. But the smaller Guggenheim Hermitage Museum remains open in the same resort. Maybe that's because casino operators have found an unexpected spin-off benefit to showcasing fine art. "This summer, we ran a free after-five [program] for locals three hours a week on Tuesday nights," museum managing director Elizabeth Herridge told the local press. As a result, she boasted, the casino reaped a new jackpot. "Every Tuesday night, they had a couple of hundred extra people signing up for player cards. We didn't expect that to be the case, but we are thrilled and so was the Venetian."

Another possible wrinkle in Vegas's future came by surprise in early October, when magician-animal tamer Roy Horn—of the world-famous Siegfried and Roy show at the Mirage—was mauled and nearly killed onstage by one one of his performing white tigers named Montecore. After the tiger clamped down on his neck, severing a vertebral artery, Horn was rushed to intensive care as he faltered near death.

Steve Wynn, who built a special theater just to house the act at the Mirage and who lavished tens of millions in salary on the duo but is no longer their employer, claimed that the tiger had not really attacked Horn, but merely got confused and was, rather brusquely, just trying to protect his master. "As Roy was leading Montecore out to the stage front on a leash," Wynn opined, "the cat became fascinated and distracted by a woman with a big hairdo in the front row. For whatever reason, Montecore was fascinated and distracted by the guest sitting ringside."

Maybe, maybe not. In either case, Roy Horn is expeced to survive, barely, but grave doubt swirls over the future of the show itself. Siegfried and Roy have a fabulously lucrative lifetime contract with MGM Mirage, but their show is now indefinitely dark. The two magicians reportedly made a pact sometime ago to never perform except as a team. If Horn is incapable of returning, how will the void be filled? Siegfried and Roy are Las Vegas's single greatest entertainment draw and produce incalculable millions not only in direct ticket sales but in tourist loyalty and goodwill. "No one's saying it yet publically," says one Mirage manager. "But if their show doesn't reopen, you can pretty much bet it's going to be replaced by some sort of sex-themed performance. Nowadays that's the only sort of thing that might come close to making the kind of money that Siegfried and Roy can haul in."

"For Las Vegas, September 11 hit on September 12" is how historian Michael Green likes to describe the economic crisis that rattled Las Vegas in the wake of the World Trade Center attacks. Spoiled by decades of uninterrupted expansion, hardly anyone in the city knew how to handle the immediate drop-off in tourism—and revenues—caused by the terrorist assualt.

But by the second anniversary of 9/11, by the fall of 2003, Las Vegas could as much as pretend the attacks had never happened. Everything that was supposed to change forever after that Tuesday morning wound up changing Las Vegas, and America's relationship with the city, only very temporarily—if at all.

On Labor Day weekend 2003, 275,000 tourists crowded into Vegas—a thousand more than on the same holiday right before the country was convulsed by the downing of the Twin Towers. Not only had tourism finally returned to pre-9/11 levels, so had the all-important tally of gambling revenues. The nearly two hundred casinos in Clark County, Nevada bagged profits of $7.75 billion during he twelve months ending June 30, 2003, a figure almost identical to the revenues of fiscal year 2001.

Las Vegas had lost two years of growth, but now seemed once again on the upward path. Tourism and gambling executives also figured that the approaching inaguration of Steve Wynn's new wonder palace in the coming year could only make things better, potenially igniting yet one more wave of frenetic expansion.

As America approached the 2004 presidential election, it seemed a nation caught in uncertainty. Uncertainty over its own secruty as well as over its role in the world. Gnawing and growing doubts persisted over how much longer U.S. troops would be in Iraq and with what purpose and at what cost. There were also worries over where American soldiers might next be sent. The national economy, America was told, was firmly and robustly recovering, but unemployment remained intolerably high, leaving college grads and their aging parents alike wondering who their next employer might be. Manufacturing jobs continued to disappear, and a million-and-a-half more Americans joined the forty-one million already without health insurance.

A conservative administration in Washington stood by its vow that massive tax cuts skewed toward the wealthy were key to economic prosperity, yet the federal budget deficit approached a record-breaking half-trillion dollars that year. That same administration watched with alarm as its once mighty popularity ratings plummeted and hovered barely above the red line of fifty percent. In California, the nation's most populous and richest state, a broad-based voters' revolt toppled the sitting governor just eleven months after his reelection. Political analysts coast-to-coast scurried to make sense of the insurgency, struggling to forecast its effects on the climaxing race for the White House.

In this perplexed and confused America, so unsure over its next step, only Las Vegas seemed to have a solid grip on its own future.

Acknowledgments

I owe thanks to many in making this book possible. I could not have understood the history of Las Vegas, let alone written a version of it, without the assistance and previous work of a number of academics and researchers much more talented than I. My greatest debt is with Michael Green of Southern Nevada Community College who not only knows more about Las Vegas than anyone I have ever met, but who so graciously, generously, and mirthfully was willing to share that knowledge.

The University of Nevada at Las Vegas is blessed with a wonderful crew of analysts and thinkers and my deepest thanks go to Bo Bernhard, Director of Gambling Studies. No one today is doing better research than he, and I was privileged to have Bo spend so much of his time with me and patiently guide me along. Also at UNLV, Eugene Moehring, David Dickens, Hal Rothman, Stowe Shoemaker, Bill Thompson, David Schwartz, and so many others offered invaluable insights. The writings of Sally Denton and Roger Morris, Mike Davis, Jack Sheehan, John L. Smith, and A.D. Hopkins were crucial to me. I can only hope to have properly interpreted their work and have accurately acknowledged all of their original research. All credit for anything enlightening in this book should go to them. I assume responsibility only for any errors and misconceptions.

Andrea Hackett put it all on the line while she helped me with this book and she took a big loss for doing so. Her revenge will be a vibrant dancers' union that one day soon will shake up and clarify the murky world of Vegas dance clubs. She's about the most capable organizer I've met anywhere. She's also a good friend.

Thanks also to Dr. Robert Hunter who continues doing God's work at the Problem Gaming Center. Paul Brown, Gary Peck, Allen Lichtenstein, and Maryann Salm helped explain local politics to me. As did Geoff Shumacher from the *Las Vegas Mercury,* David Hare from *CityLife,* and the irrepressible Steve Miller. Nick Kallos at the Casino Gaming School provided a delightful encounter as did Sam Smith at the Native Son bookstore. Thanks also to Uri Clinton and Stan Armstrong. Bill Friedman is a casino genius. Brother David Buer of the Franciscan order should one day be canonized for his work with the Vegas homeless.

Kenny Franks has become a special friend and never ceases to amaze me with his encyclopedic memory. A toke also to Jackie, Mel, Henry, Hyun, Rick, Subi, and so many others who have made my table "research" at Binion's such an ongoing if not always profitable pleasure. Ziggy at the Mandalay Bay is the best dealer I've ever met and was also overly generous with his time. Howard Schwartz at the Gamblers Book Club should charge admission—he's a gentleman, scholar, and a great wit. I also owe much to Max

Rubin, including a radically improved game of Blackjack. The unofficial Mayor of Mandalay Bay, Howard Klein, was very kind to me and is a true asset to Las Vegas. Louie at the Liberty Café told me some great stories and serves up the best four-in-the-morning sympathy along with his world-class ham and eggs. Michael Kaplan, one of the best gambling writers in America, offered some important transcontinental assistance. Elaine Sanchez in Mayor Goodman's office was very helpful and the mayor was gracious with his time. I wish Frank Wright, former curator of the Nevada State Historical Society and Museum, had survived to read this book. Everyone who has ever met him was pained by his passing.

Very special thanks go to my colleagues and editors who also generously supported this project (and cut me plenty of slack so I could finish it). Thanks for the understanding and ongoing support from *Nation* magazine editor Katrina vanden Heuvel and publisher Victor Navasky. Thanks also to Senior Editor Karen Rothmyer. Much gratitude also to all my colleagues at the Nation Institute including executive director Taya Grobow and president Hamilton Fish III.

At the *L.A. Weekly,* editor-in-chief Laurie Ochoa has given support above and beyond. Thanks also to the *Weekly's* Alan Mittelstaedt, John Powers, Joe Donnelly, and Sharan Street, as well as to David Schneiderman of *Village Voice Media* for their support. Sue Horton at the *Los Angeles Times* allowed me to preview some key concepts of this book in her fine Sunday Opinion section. Steve Montiel, executive director of the Institute for Justice and Journalism at USC's Annenberg School for Communication has also helped me find the time to write this book.

Numerous friends and writers served as sounding boards and providers of moral encouragement. Thanks to Tim Frasca, Arianna Huffington, Patrick Caddell, Joe Domanick, Greg Goldin, David Corn, William Bradley, and Micah Sifry for their duties. The brilliant Ben Schwarz at the *Atlantic Monthly* inspired whole sections of this book. Kathy Lo, Limor Ben Cohen, and Mark Schubb are all fellow admirers of the Desert Inn and assisted me with the early field research on this project.

My sister Bonnie Spolin served as adviser on All Things Rat Pack. Thanks to my parents for dragging me to El Rancho Vegas before I could walk (and Mom, wherever you are, you really should start hitting those twelves).

This book was the brainchild of Carl Bromley, editorial director of Nation Books. Thanks, Carl, for making me envision the book and then allowing me to write it. Ruth Baldwin, thank you for your deft ability to impose such stern discipline and make sure it really got written.

My family makes it all worth it. I've got a Full House of love and support from Patricia and Natasha. With their support and strength, I'm always a winner.